BRENDAN

BY RONAN NOONE

DRAMATISTS
PLAY SERVICE
INC.

BRENDAN
Copyright © 2009, Ronan Noone

All Rights Reserved

SPECIAL NOTE

Anyone receiving permission to produce BRENDAN is required to give credit to the Author as sole and exclusive Author of the Play on the title page of all programs distributed in connection with performances of the Play and in all instances in which the title of the Play appears for purposes of advertising, publicizing or otherwise exploiting the Play and/or a production thereof. The name of the Author must appear on a separate line, in which no other name appears, immediately beneath the title and in size of type equal to 50% of the size of the largest, most prominent letter used for the title of the Play. No person, firm or entity may receive credit larger or more prominent than that accorded the Author. The following acknowledgment must appear on the title page in all programs distributed in connection with performances of the Play:

BRENDAN was originally produced by the Huntington Theatre Company, Boston, Nicholas Martin, Artistic Director; Michael Maso, Managing Director.

For Lizzie Roche

BRENDAN had its premiere with the Huntington Theatre Company (Nicholas Martin, Artistic Director; Michael Maso, Managing Director) at the Calderwood Pavilion, in Boston, Massachusetts, on October 24, 2007. It was directed by Justin Waldman; the set design was by Alexander Dodge; the costume design was by Mariann Verheyen; the lighting design was by Jeff Croiter; the sound design was by Fitz Patton; the production stage manager was Eileen Ryan Kelly; and the stage manager was Kelly Beaulieu. The cast was as follows:

BRENDAN .... Dashiell Eaves
WOMAN .... Nancy E. Carroll
ROSE .... Natalie Gold
MARIA .... Kelly McAndrew
DAISY, REGISTRY GIRL, ASHLING .... Kathleen McElfresh
DECLAN, VICTOR .... Tommy Schrider
FRED, STATE COP .... Cliff Odle
STEVEO, SOUTHIE SALESMAN,
VANDAL, COURT OFFICER .... Ciaran Crawford
JUDGE, BUM, HOUSE OWNER .... Bradley Thoennes

A special note of mention to Boston University School of Theatre's New Play Initiative, through which this play received a full developmental student production.

CHARACTERS

BRENDAN, 30 — Irish
WOMAN, 60 — Irish
ROSE, 30 — American
MARIA, 35 — American
DAISY, 30 — Irish
DECLAN, 40 — Irish
VICTOR, 40 — American
FRED, 50 — African-American
STEVEO, 30 — Irish
ASHLING, STATE COP, REGISTRY MAN, SOUTHIE SALESMAN, VANDAL, COURT OFFICER, JUDGE, BUM, HOUSE OWNER

PLACE

Boston.

TIME

Now.

A NOTE ON THE SET: It could be staged with minimal props or as a large pullout street set, either way there should be a concentration on an operatic/balletic style, using the cast as street scene characters, courtroom, bar room, etc., where appropriate throughout the play.

Accordingly, the transitions from one scene to another should be fluid.

A NOTE ON DOUBLING AND TRIPLING: Although, at this stage, I have never seen a full production of this play with just seven actors, I think it may be possible under these circumstances:

BRENDAN, 30

WOMAN, 60

ROSE, 30

MARIA/DAISY/ASHLING, 30

STEVEO/SALESMAN/VANDAL, 30

FRED/JUDGE 2/BUM/COURT OFFICER/STATE COP/ REGISTRY MAN, 50

DECLAN/VICTOR/JUDGE 1/HOUSE OWNER, 40

BRENDAN

Scene 1

Mother's Dead

A light turns. Brendan is reading a letter. He is in his under-wear. Shirt off. Boots on. He drops the letter to the ground. He taps his Budweiser bottle with his harmonica like a conductor with the baton. We hear the first low strains of the music. We are introduced to the characters through street scenes as he begins to conduct. It is Carmina Burana. *Music stops. In silhouette in the back we hear —*

ASHLING. Dear Brendan, Mammy died last week, and we buried her three days ago. She wouldn't let me tell you until after she was buried, and that was her way. You know yourself. Since we don't have a phone number for you, I could only let you know by letter. *(Music again. It stops, as we see the growing anxiety in Brendan.)* It was a great turnout by the village, and even the harmonica orchestra from national school played at the graveside. Their teacher, Danny Tobin, who you went to school with, organized the boys to play the "Barcarole." I remember when you used to play that on the harmonica and Mammy used to say it was her favourite tune, even more than anything by Dean Martin. *(Music again, as he conducts — but falters again.)* I'm sorry you weren't there, and I know you know we understand, but we missed you, and I still miss you. Little Shayme is ten now and looks like you, and Maurice is still at the factory and everyone was asking for you. I think they understood why you didn't come home, and what is it to them, either? Michael Harpy told everyone you were in Memphis with Elvis. *(He turns around. His back to the audience. He conducts more furiously now.*

Then stops.) Write sometime, will you. I have to go now and take the sheets in off the line. It's going to rain. Your loving sister, Ashling. *(It stops again. He looks at the letter on the ground and the letter box.)* P.S. Judy is married now and living in the city. You'd never see her anymore. I thought you might like to know. I know Mammy would never mention it. *(Music again, and Brendan continues to conduct as the characters dissipate; finally he collapses in submission. The Woman lights her cigarette as a light comes up on her.)*

WOMAN. Well. *(She walks into the scene, audaciously.)*

BRENDAN. *(Surprised.)* Well.

WOMAN. Well. *(Looking at the letter on the box.)* Your sister wrote a nice letter about me. She didn't have to mention that Judy two-penny hussy.

BRENDAN. Don't start.

WOMAN. All I'm sayin' …

BRENDAN. Don't start.

WOMAN. She was a hussy.

BRENDAN. Come on.

WOMAN. The state she left you in — *(Brendan takes a drink from his bottle.)* You're drinking a lot, I see?

BRENDAN. *(Exasperated.)* Je-sus Chr-ist. *(Brendan puts the letter in the box.)*

WOMAN. You keep all my letters in that box, too?

BRENDAN. I do.

WOMAN. You didn't completely forget me, then. *(Pause.)* Have you found a nice American girl for yourself?

BRENDAN. *(Putting on a jacket.)* No.

WOMAN. Where are you going?

BRENDAN. Out.

WOMAN. Out where?

BRENDAN. Out out?

WOMAN. Brush your hair before you go, Brendan, love.

BRENDAN. I won't.

WOMAN. *(Soft and loaded with guilt.)* That's no way to talk to your mother. *(Brendan leaves the apartment. The Woman follows him from here on out.)*

Scene 2

The Boss

BRENDAN. *(All of his continuing letter to Ashling is directed to the audience.)* Dear Ashling, The first thing you smell is coffee and then petrol, gas, and from then on you can't distinguish between the two, and that's the smell of America. You step outside the airport and the warm air hits you like a blast from a furnace, and you know things are going to be awful different. I got in one of the yellow cabs, and I went downtown and found the nearest Irish bar. How Irish is that — come all this way just to find a bar. *(Fred walks by — fifty, black.)*
FRED. You an asshole
BRENDAN. *(Turns.)* What?
FRED. What, what you mean what — ? *(Walking offstage.)*
BRENDAN. What I do? *(Fred turning around.)*
FRED. Ya don't know — do ya?
BRENDAN. I wouldn't ask if I did, Fred?
FRED. How long you working for me?
BRENDAN. Two years.
FRED. You an asshole *(Fred walks offstage. Brendan enters the bar.)*

Scene 3

Griffin's Pub

Declan, Irish, thirty, the barman, appears up from behind the counter. Declan is a small fella.

DECLAN. So Fred's wife came by the paint job the other morning looking for him. And you told her Fred took off.
BRENDAN. Yeah.

9

DECLAN. And now she wants to know where he was, and he's gettin' a ration a shite for it. Coz you didn't cover for him. *(Laughs.)*
WOMAN. Dear Brendan,
DECLAN. And I said, no surprise there, Fred, coz Brendan is a bollocks.
WOMAN. Mammy died last week —
DECLAN. Do you hear me? *(Laughs.)*
WOMAN. And we buried her three days ago.
DECLAN. Hey. What's the matter with ya?
BRENDAN. Give me a beer.
DECLAN. Oh, that's Yank talk now — "Give me a beer." What kinda a "beer" would you like, "guy"?
BRENDAN. Declan, just give me a Bud? Please.
DECLAN. I'm only messing with you, Smiler. *(In walks a Bum. Declan ignores him. The Bum looks around and then begins dancing an Irish jig. Exaggerated steps with a big smile, all the while singing the diddly-I Irish music, whooping and hollering as he goes along. Brendan watches happily — it takes his mind off. Declan shakes his head. Bum stops, comes to the bar.)*
BUM. *(Declan ignores him.)* That's my Irish jig, buddy, and I'm sayin' it's worth a drink. Yeah. *(Smiles.)*
BRENDAN. I got called up for my citizenship ceremony.
DECLAN. Good for you. That'll never happen to me coz I'm just going to keep collecting my greenbacks and then piss off home. This place annoys me.
BRENDAN. Why the hell are you here, then?
DECLAN. I just told you, ya deaf prick. Is Steveo, "your chauffeur," gonna drive you to the ceremony? *(Bum raps at the bar.)*
BRENDAN. What'd ya mean?
DECLAN. Steveo, you know, the person you use to drive your arse from job to job.
BRENDAN. He just gives me a lift to work. *(Bum raps at the bar, louder.)*
DECLAN. Your personal driver.
BRENDAN. Do you do anything but annoy the hell out of people? He's not my personal driver.
DECLAN. *(To Bum.)* I'm not serving you. *(Brendan starts swallowing his beer down. It's soured now.)*
BUM. Why not?
DECLAN. Coz you're drunk.

BUM. I'm not. That's why I'm here.

BRENDAN. Do domething decent and give him a drink.

BUM. I'd like a drink please, Mick.

DECLAN. Well, that certainly ain't going to help your cause. *(Brendan gets up to go.)*

BUM. Mr. Bartender. A word please.

DECLAN. *(To Brendan.)* Where you going? *(To Bum.)* What? *(Bum grabs Declan by the lapels, pulls him over the counter and throws him on the ground. To Brendan in panic:)* Brendan! *(Bum begins kicking Declan. Brendan looks on. He doesn't get involved.)*

BUM. I fought in two friggin' wars, and I'd like a drink in my own country. Ya still think I'm drunk? A little respect, ya Mick. *(Bum drops Declan to the ground. He looks at Brendan, who steps aside.)* I'm not even thirsty now. *(The Bum picks up his quarters, and he exits. Declan is left on the ground, Declan is bleeding.)*

WOMAN. She wouldn't let me tell you until after she was buried, and that was her way —

DECLAN. *(Interrupting, to Brendan:)* Why didn't ya help me, ya bolix?

BRENDAN. I don't know why — maybe coz you deserved it.

DECLAN. What?

BRENDAN. You heard me?

DECLAN. Get out. I'm closing.

BRENDAN. Gladly

DECLAN. I'm closing up.

BRENDAN. I heard ya. *(Brendan goes to exit.)*

DECLAN. Get out. *(Brendan exits Griffin's pub.)*

BRENDAN. *(Letter.)* I got a job cleaning dishes in another Irish bar called The Swinging Paddy, and they had a wooden sign outside of a leprechaun in his little green jacket with a noose around his neck, and he was dangling over a shiny pot of gold, and his arms, like elastic, trying to touch the pot … and for some reason, even though he couldn't reach the gold, he had a big smile on his face. I remember asking the boss, if you're here long enough is that what it feels like, but he said no. "It's just a wooden sign to make us look more Irish."

Scene 4

Daisy is Upset

As Brendan turns — Daisy McGuire, Irish, makes her way to exit as she shouts offstage.

DAISY. Ya fuck ya, ya fuckin' fuck. *(Sees Brendan. She pauses.)* Hi, Smiler. *(Tears rolling down her face.)*
BRENDAN. Bad night?
DAISY. You could say that
BRENDAN. It's going around
DAISY. *(Shouts offstage to Steveo.)* Leave me alone. Ya "feck sake," you too. *(To Brendan.)* I have to go, Smiler. *(Brendan watches her leave. She hides and watches Steveo enter — Irish, rough, ready and funny.)*
STEVEO. *(To Brendan.)* She gone?
BRENDAN. Daisy?
STEVEO. No. Ma feckin' donna.
BRENDAN. I think so.
STEVEO. Stay clear of women, Brendan. Ya can't trust them, ya know — they're born to drive you feckin' mad, you know — ya ya ya ya ya ya ya give them all ya can — and they still want more — I feckin', feckin', feckin' feck don't know, ya know — ya know — fuck it— *(Walks offstage. Steveo exits. Brendan watches him as he leaves. He sits on the bench.)*
WOMAN. Your friends have a lovely way of expressing themselves, Brendan.

Scene 5

Walking Daisy Home

Daisy comes out of hiding and enters, smoking. Brendan doesn't want a conversation.

DAISY. Hey, Smiler. *(She sits.)*
BRENDAN. Yeah. Hi, Daisy. *(He looks away.)*
DAISY. I had a fight with Steveo, Smiler.
BRENDAN. I I I kinda thought that.
DAISY. Would ya mind walking me home, coz …
BRENDAN. Oh yeah. Yeah. Can I ask you something?
DAISY. Yeah.
BRENDAN. Would it be okay if you didn't call me Smiler, coz …
DAISY. Oh no problem. I'm sorry. I didn't know …
BRENDAN. Brendan is fine.
DAISY. Brendan, I know. Thanks, Brendan, for walking me home. I'm not taking you from some girl?
BRENDAN. No. No.
DAISY. Are you sure?
BRENDAN. No. I was just walking home. *(Pause.)* How are you enjoying America?
DAISY. Ah, it's alright. Steveo was helping me adjust but now the honeymoon period *is over.* When were you home last?
BRENDAN. Five years.
DAISY. Wow. Declan told me about the girl ya had back home—
WOMAN. Judy.
BRENDAN. What girl?
DAISY. I don't know. I shouldn't have said that. I was trying to make conversation.
WOMAN. The two-penny hussy.
BRENDAN. What else did he say?
DAISY. It doesn't matter. *(Brendan looks at her.)* Well, he says it didn't work out, you and the girl …
BRENDAN. Yeah.

13

DAISY. And ya went up a mountain or something, and you took a pile a Tylenol. *(Pause.)* I think there's something so romantic about that. To try and kill yourself and all — for love. Declan thinks you were crazy to do that. He says your mother found ya up there. But he doesn't understand, love. And he doesn't like women. All he wants to do is ride ya and leave ya. Bolix. You know. He doesn't understand. Steveo is afraid to love too. That's his problem. Most men … I'm sorry, Brendan. I shouldn't have said it. I was only saying to have someone love ya that much … *(Daisy knows to say no more.)*
BRENDAN. It was Advil, not Tylenol, you know.
DAISY. Ohhh — *(We hear the low strains of Verdi's "Anvil Chorus" building. The Woman goes to sit on the armchair.)*
WOMAN. Hello, Brendan — It's now a week since you left and it's as much like yesterday or as if you never existed it's been so long.
DAISY. Are you going to go back home ever?
BRENDAN. This is home. I'll leave you here, if that's —
DAISY. Brendan. Listen. I didn't mean —
BRENDAN. *(Strained and stressed but soft.)* It's okay.
WOMAN. It's left my heart very empty, but I know we did the right thing. You frightened me, Brendan. *(He begins walking away.)*
DAISY. Brendan, I wish Steveo could love like that, you know.
BRENDAN. Sure.

Scene 6

Another Letter and Rose

Brendan pours himself a whiskey.

WOMAN. You frightened us all. There was nothing here for you.
BRENDAN. *(Frustration.)* Aaaahahaahah. *(He turns up the music to try and drown her out.)*
WOMAN. The weather is nice at the moment. A couple of days of sunshine this week. And the rain was soft and came off the sea like a mist. *(As she recites, he pulls out a section of a free alternative newspaper, which is beside a small harmonica. The paper is advertising sex. We see*

a big-busted, half-naked woman on the cover. He reads through it. He puts it down. He finds his tattered personal phone book; picks up the phone. Changes his mind. He starts playing his harmonica, badly. "The Star-Spangled Banner." He drinks his whiskey and pours another. Music hits its chorus and she speaks louder to be heard. Brendan plays the harmonica louder.) Brendan, I just wanted to say we all do the best we can. We make friends when we can make friends, and we love even when we can't help it. Some people are lonely and some people are happy, but we're all the same, and as long as we are good, just a good person then we're alright. We're alright. Anyway, say a prayer every day, and I love you very much. Mammy. Write, please. *(There is a knocking at the door. And then another loud knock. Slowly, he wipes his nose with his sleeve, turns down the music and opens the door. There is a pretty American girl, thirty-one. Rose. She has a port-wine scar covering some of her face.)*

ROSE. Hello. I just moved in downstairs. Could you keep your music down?

BRENDAN. Oh, I'm sorry. I'm sorry.

ROSE. It's two A.M. And I'm working in the morning.

BRENDAN. I'm sorry.

ROSE. It's okay. It was just a little loud. *(Beat.)* By the way, I'm Rose. Since I see you around. I've seen you in the Stop & Shop.

BRENDAN. I'm Brendan. I've seen you around, too. You, you work there?

ROSE. Yeah, but I just moved in here and *(The Woman stands up.)*

WOMAN. Apologise again.

BRENDAN. I'm sorry. I really am — aah — *(Pause.)*

ROSE. It's fine. Okay then. Thank you. You have a nice smile, Brendan. *(She goes. He closes the door.)*

WOMAN. You do have a nice smile, Brendan.

BRENDAN. Will ya leave me alone?

WOMAN. That poor thing must be driven demented with that mark on her face. Not easy for a woman, you know. A woman values the way she looks, and then to be cursed with — *(Brendan finishes the whiskey.)* One or two is enough, Brendan, otherwise it's a problem. Your father. He had a problem. Don't get me wrong. He was able to handle it. Wonder would ya be here if he hadn't gone so young.

BRENDAN. Ah, God's sake. *(He picks up the phone and calls the number he found in his book.)* Hello … yes Maria … If tomorrow would be okay … Yes … That's okay. Grand … Yes, grand, grand.

Eight. *(A sexy woman walks by. Steveo enters with his car. He is in his painting garb. He watches her pass.)*
STEVEO. *(Shouts.)* Hoo haa — Did ya see the ass on that thing?
WOMAN. Who were you ringing? *(Brendan walks away.)*

Scene 7

Driving with Steveo

Brendan approaches.

STEVEO. Alright wasn't it?
BRENDAN. Yeah, it was a nice ass.
STEVEO. *(Laughing.)* You're some tosspot, Smiler.
WOMAN. *(Still in her armchair.)* Mammy died last week, and we buried her three days ago. She wouldn't let me tell you until —
STEVEO. *(Cuts her off.)* What's wrong with ya?
WOMAN. She wouldn't let me tell —
STEVEO. Here, were you talking to Daisy last night?
BRENDAN. Well no, I mean, I walked … She said you and her —
STEVEO. Says she's up the pole. Preggers. Bolix.
BRENDAN. With you?
STEVEO. Yeah, Brendan. Why, did you hear something else? Feck sake. My parents are comin' in from Ireland tonight, too.
BRENDAN. I didn't know you were going out with her.
STEVEO. That's coz your head's up your arse. Feck sake. Three months. And I like her too. But I'm not ready. I want to ride a few more before I settle.
BRENDAN. She's a nice girl.
STEVEO. I know she's a feckin' nice girl.
BRENDAN. Parents coming. That's good. Right?
STEVEO. They'll hit the fecking roof if they find out I got someone up the pole.
BRENDAN. Oh.
STEVEO. Oh! So you'll have to find another way to get to work. I'm takin' time off from work to show them around.

BRENDAN. Yeah, okay. (*The Woman joins him. It feels now she is more permanently with him.*)
STEVEO. Time you bought a car, Brendan. Look at my beauty.
WOMAN. They're dangerous. And in America. Other side of the road. I don't want anything to happen to you.
BRENDAN. You never want anything to happen to me.
STEVEO. Who?
BRENDAN. Nothing.
STEVEO. Have you got Tourette's all of a sudden?
BRENDAN. What? No … No …
STEVEO. You're nothing in America without a car. Get in the car.
WOMAN. I'm going with you.
BRENDAN. What?
STEVEO. (*Louder.*) Get in the car.
WOMAN. I'm going with you.
BRENDAN. Jesus —
WOMAN. Stop cursing. (*Steveo drives aggressively. Brendan is used to this. Woman is in the back seat, nervous. She pops her head between them as they drive.*) I'd love a car, by right.
STEVEO. Why don't ya buy one? You should have by now. Jesus! (*To an unseen other car.*) Get out of it, ya dopey feck. (*To Brendan.*) Did ya see that?
BRENDAN. I did.
STEVEO. Dopey feckin' feck. Did ya see it? (*Brendan is holding on to the roof handle, tight.*)
BRENDAN. Hard to miss it, in fairness. How long are the parents staying?
STEVEO. TOSSPOT. (*Beat.*) Two weeks. Want to do some shopping. Levi jeans.
BRENDAN. Levi's.
WOMAN. I like Levi's.
STEVEO. Oh aye, feckin' cost nothing over here compared to there. Levi feckin' jeans.
BRENDAN. Levi jeans.
STEVEO. I haven't seen them in three years. Can ya believe it. Three feckin' years.
BRENDAN. That's a while.
STEVEO. If I had a green card, like you, I'd have hopped over the ocean three or four times by now. Instead of pining like a feckin' egit over here.

BRENDAN. Ireland's rich now. You could still go back.
STEVEO. Ah. I'm happy here. I made a life for meself — not listening to me family telling me what to do. Anyway I like the feckin' sunshine — When is the citizenship ceremony?
BRENDAN. Next week.
STEVEO. I'm going to the ceremony that day. We'll have a great piss-up. Maybe you could marry me, with all the gay laws, hah? Make me legal, hah. Feckin' yeah.
BRENDAN. Maybe.
STEVEO. Jesus, Brendan, all these years driving you, you have to lighten up. You're wound like a Swiss clock. *(They get out of the car and:)*
BRENDAN. Are you going to tell the parents about Daisy?
STEVEO. I am in my feckin' shite. *(Steveo starts to climb a ladder to paint.)*
BRENDAN. *(Letter.)* After doing the dishes for a few months, they put me waitering because they were short-staffed, and it was great, at first, because I made the tips. And my accent, which I think makes me sound like a bogtrotter — well the Yanks love it, and they were tipping me extra just to say the word "Spuds." Then I'd have to put it in a sentence for them — like "spuds are delicious." But I started feeling like a clown so I packed it in and got a job painting houses instead.

Scene 8

House Painting

Steven is hanging off the edge of a ladder trying to reach an overhang with his brush.

WOMAN. Tell Steven to be careful, Brendan.
BRENDAN. Be careful, Steven. We'll move the ladder, and we'll get it later.
STEVEO. FECK IT. I'll get it now.
WOMAN. It's foul language that makes us indistinguishable from

farm animals. *(We watch with trepidation as Steveo paints the piece. Steveo gets it. Relief. An older WASP-y man comes out of the house.)*
STEVEO. Feckin' feck.
HOUSE OWNER. Excuse me. I have neighbors. Could you please refrain from the language.
WOMAN. What did I tell you?
BRENDAN. I'm sorry, sir. *(Steven looks down.)*
HOUSE OWNER. I'll get a more professional company.
BRENDAN. Won't happen again. *(He turns around, and Steven sticks his finger up at him and nearly falls off the ladder again.)*
STEVEO. "I have neighbours. Could you —"
BRENDAN. Ssh, ssh, come down. *(Fred enters.)*
FRED. What's wrong?
BRENDAN. Nothing, Fred.
STEVEO. Fine, boss. *(To Brendan.)* You gettin' lunch? *(Climbing down the ladder.)*
BRENDAN. No, I brought me usual. *(Steveo exits. Brendan unpacks his lunch. The Woman, beside him, watching.)*
FRED. Brendan, I wanted to say …
BRENDAN. I just wanted to say, well, Declan said that I got ya in trouble with your wife, and I didn't mean —
FRED. Doesn't matter.
BRENDAN. I didn't know. That's why you called me an asshole.
FRED. Drop it.
BRENDAN. I didn't know that —
FRED. Brendan, I take off every Tuesday at the same time, and you didn't know.
WOMAN. Leave him alone, you.
BRENDAN. I forgot it was Tuesday.
FRED. It's alright, never mind. Go on back. By the way you'll have to find a way to get to work, if you want to stay with me. Steveo told you about his parents coming over?
BRENDAN. I know. I'm going to buy a car. I'm going to learn to drive.
FRED. Good. Because you'll need your own transportation.
WOMAN. *(Following him.)* Aaaah, Brendan, I'm worried —
BRENDAN. *(Letter. Cutting Woman off.)* I found an apartment close to the bar I worked in, on Pine Street. I was sharing with a couple of Irish girls from Dublin. And they were always trying to get me to come out and party, but I was afraid to go out because I kept think-

ing about what an arse I made of myself trying to kill myself because of Judy and how messed up I was. I thought that was love, you know. Jesus, Ashling, I embarrassed you all terribly. *(We hear the low strains of Mozart's "Laudate Dominum" — Requiem — from the car radio.)*

Scene 9

Driving Home

Steveo is watching Brendan conduct and imitating him while the music is playing.

STEVEO. What kind of music is this —
BRENDAN. It's nice music.
STEVEO. It's shite.
BRENDAN. It's Mozart.
STEVEO. Feck Mozart. *(He changes the music station.)* YEahhaaahh — Yeahahah — Yeahhhaaa *(Changes the music to a hard rock station. A car nearly hits them. He steers off.)* I swear to feck, Brendan, the feckin' tosspots. I'll feckin' ram that Chevrolet up their fecking arses. I'm feckin' telling you, Brendan. Feckin American drivers, the drivers around here are feckin' diabolical. *(Giving the finger out the window. Brendan turns off the music.)* Come on, ya little bastard *(Calm now. It is delightfully bipolar.)* What are you doing tonight?
BRENDAN. I'm walking over to the Stop & Shop. I've got to pick up a few things.
STEVEO. Listen, after the parents leave, I could give you a few lessons. Teach you how to drive.
BRENDAN. Oh, I'd appreciate that.
STEVEO. "Appreciate," listen to ya. All Americanised.
BRENDAN. I could pay you more than the gas money I give you.
STEVEO. We're feckin' friends, Brendan. You don't have to pay me for feckin' everything. You know, its feckin' friendship.
BRENDAN. I'd like to pay you.
STEVEO. Feckin' whatever. Anyway I'm off to the airport, pick

them up. I'll see ya in the morning.
BRENDAN. I thought you were on vacation.
STEVEO. I told Fred the wanker I'd do a half day, that's it.
BRENDAN. Okay.
STEVEO. And don't mention anyone about Daisy, right?
BRENDAN. Oh no, I wouldn't.
STEVEO. You know, I'll probably end up marrying her, feck sake. Anyway, I'm gone. *(Steveo lazily salutes him. Then we hear him shout as he drives off.)* Yahoooo.
WOMAN. That was nice of Steven to offer to teach you. If you just cut his tongue out, he'd be a lovely fella.

Scene 10

Apology with Chocolates

Brendan is carrying chocolates. He knocks at Rose's door. He knocks again, and Rose opens it.

BRENDAN. Hello.
ROSE. Hello.
BRENDAN. I just wanted to apologise for last night, and to apologise, and to give you these as a token of apology as a sorry, for, you know. I didn't mean. *(Rose hesitates.)*
ROSE. You know it was just late and —
BRENDAN. No, I know it was. I turned it up too loud because, well because —
ROSE. It's okay, *(She takes the chocolates, notices the name on them.)*
BRENDAN. And they are Rose's chocolates. Like your name.
ROSE. The chocolates.
BRENDAN. Yes, they're called "Rose's." They're from where I'm from.
ROSE. From upstairs.
BRENDAN. No, I mean —
ROSE. I know, I was just kidding.
BRENDAN. So you work at the Stop & Shop?

ROSE. I do. I'm the new manager.
BRENDAN. Oh, I just saw your picture on the way out the other day. It looks nice.
ROSE. Thank you. I'm actually running out the door to go to work.
BRENDAN. Oh, I'm sorry. I was just going —
ROSE. But …
BRENDAN. Yes?
ROSE. Ireland, right? I love your accent.
BRENDAN. Thanks. I like your accent, too.
ROSE. Thank you for the chocolates. (*He smiles. She closes the door.*)
WOMAN. (*Laughing.*) Knockin' the woman right off her feet. "I like your accent too." Oh couldn't you have said something about her smile or her hair? Her accent, and an American accent too, ohh.
BRENDAN. I thought I did a nice thing.
WOMAN. I'm sorry. I'm sorry. You're right. It was. It was a lovely thing. I'm just anxious for you to be happy.
BRENDAN. I am happy.
WOMAN. You're not.
BRENDAN. Well, neither are you. Otherwise you wouldn't be here. (*Maria's apartment. She is a woman, thirty-five. Attractive. She is rambunctious and urban. We hear the low tones of hip-hop.*)
MARIA. Brendan, baby, come on in.
WOMAN. Why won't ya tell anyone about me? Where are you going?
BRENDAN. To get rid of my stress.
MARIA. Say hello, baby.

Scene 11

Maria the Prostitute

BRENDAN. Hello.
MARIA. I love that hello of yours. Say it again.
BRENDAN. Ah, hello.
MARIA. That's it. You're so cute.
WOMAN. What is this place?
MARIA. You know something, Brendan?

BRENDAN. What?

MARIA. You're my favorite.

BRENDAN. Grand.

MARIA. "Grand." Stop it, you'll have me wetting myself and I haven't touched ya.

BRENDAN. Where? *(He takes out some money. She offers her cleavage.)*

MARIA. Oh, just leave it there. A little drinky before?

BRENDAN. Yes, please. *(Looking around.)* Did ya paint the place?

MARIA. I did. *(Still feeling the walls. She hands him a whiskey.)*

BRENDAN. I like the trim. It's a good job.

MARIA. It'd want to be. I paid through me arms and legs for it.

BRENDAN. Yeah.

MARIA. You're the best-looking man that ever crossed my threshold, but you might be the most confused as well. *(Brendan starts touching the trim around the wall.)*

BRENDAN. It's a nice job alright *(He drinks it all down.)*

MARIA. *(To his speed drinking.)* Whoa, cowboy. Why you always play so coy. My little virgin. I have a lot of affection for you, Brendan. I taught you, and I was glad doing it. You're like my big Irish bear. *(Brendan roars gently at her. She laughs at him. He smiles.)* I've got some smooth hip-hop, and I'd like to work with that this week. Is that alright? I know you like the classical.

BRENDAN. It's fine. No.

MARIA. I got rid of Barry White. Clients were starting to drool on me. Getting all slurpy. Now it's hip-hop, good music to fuck to. *(Woman moves closer — coming to terms with the place. Superior.)*

WOMAN. Well isn't that nice! *(Pause.)*

BRENDAN. Hip-hop is fine. *(We hear hip-hop beat. Brendan feels the paint on the wall. Maria takes off her robe. Maria is in a Victoria's Secret getup, looking cheap, trashy and sexy. Skin is squeezing its way out. Brendan is undressing to his y-fronts. White.)*

MARIA. We really have to get you some new underwear.

BRENDAN. You don't like these.

MARIA. Come here. *(Maria pulls him close and puts her head in his crotch and starts —)*

WOMAN. *(Shocked.)* Oh — Your father would love to see this. Oh — He'd love it. *(Brendan is feeling more and more awkward as this progresses. Brendan goes to take Maria's bra off. He is all over the place, trying to ignore his mother and be his own man. He can't.)*

MARIA. What's wrong with you, baby? *(He becomes more and*

more anxious. Brendan looks around at Woman.)
WOMAN. Oh yes, your father would love to see you having SEX.
MARIA. Are you alright?
WOMAN. Lots of sex. *(He stops.)*
BRENDAN. I have to go.
MARIA. A little performance anxiety. Don't worry.
WOMAN. Tons of sex. *(Brendan pulls on his pants and shirt.)*
BRENDAN. I have to go.
MARIA. What's the matter.
WOMAN. Oral sex
BRENDAN. I'm not feeling right. *(He exits quickly.)*
WOMAN. This is grieving for your mother, American-style. Isn't it? Hah. Hah. Hah. Oh it's marvelous — MARVELOUS show of RESPECT.

Scene 12

Looking at the Cars Passing

Brendan is on the street outside. The Woman is standing over him.

BRENDAN. Okay, enough — don't say any more.
WOMAN. *(Her foot tapping.)* I don't know what to say. I can say I'm ashamed — I can say I'm ashamed — Oh, I can, and that makes me feel much better — I'm ashamed. Oh yeah. And what about — AIDS. OH MY GOD — AIDS. You could get AIDS — I won't mention it again. That'll be the last of it. Agreed. Agreed — It's the last of it. Agreed. *(Pause.)* Are you listening to me?
BRENDAN. It's hard to ignore ya.
WOMAN. What are you looking at?
BRENDAN. Cars driving by.
WOMAN. Oh, Brendan, I'm afraid of you driving cars. *(Brendan gets up.)* Where you going?
BRENDAN. Bed. Steveo's picking me up for work in the morning.
WOMAN. Are we agreed on ... the other thing? *(Brendan is*

standing at the stoop, waiting for Steveo.)
BRENDAN. *(Letter.)* The first few years here, Ashling and I'd see people walking down the street and they'd remind me of people from home. They'd just look like them. You know. It was kinda strange. It kept bringing me back to where I came from. Like your mind was trying to adjust by making people you didn't know look like people you knew, so your mind could understand where it was. Mad isn't it. Anyway, I saw someone who looked like Danny Tobin one day, and then out of nowhere I remembered playing under fourteens football with Danny years ago on the Silver Strand pitch. It was a nice memory.

Scene 13

Steveo Pick Up

Brendan checks his watch. Steveo is late. He sees Daisy.

WOMAN. Nice morning. Where's this driver friend of yours?
DAISY. Hi, Brendan. You waiting for Steveo?
BRENDAN. He's late. Normally he's on time.
DAISY. I just came from the hospital, Brendan. *(She starts crying. Brendan is blank.)* He crashed into the railings on the way to the airport. He's dead, Brendan.
BRENDAN. What?
WOMAN. Oooh.
BRENDAN. What about his parents? *(She looks for a hug, but Brendan doesn't know how to be intimate. Barely discernible is his grief. But it's there in immensity. They stand looking at each other.)* His parents?
DAISY. They're at the morgue, and his mother won't leave. It was her first time in America.
WOMAN. Do they have a place to stay?
BRENDAN. Do they have a place to stay?
DAISY. Declan in the bar got the call from them at the airport coz they hadn't seen Steven. He always said ring the bar if they were

looking for him. He was always cautious of immigration. He's gone, Brendan. *(Pause.)* I didn't know him long, but I knew him long enough to fall for him. *(She puts her arms around him. Brendan looks very awkward. He wants to put his arms around her, but he can't. The letter box is open. He squeezes his harmonica. We hear "Ebben? Ne andrò lontana" from* La Wally, *by Alfredo Catalani.)*
WOMAN. Hello Brendan, You're gone two years now. I know I told you not to return ever and that it would be better for you to concentrate on making something of yourself.
DAISY. They're bringing his coffin to the airport tomorrow.

Scene 14

Another Letter from Home

Brendan at the bar. The music is heard.

WOMAN. Them were the hardest words I ever said, and I meant them, but I don't want you dwelling on them and thinking me harsh. Brendan, I think you think I was, and that's why you don't contact me. *(Brendan is having a whiskey.)*
BRENDAN. Your sister comes and looks in on me *(While the Woman talks, Brendan drinks down the whiskey and pours another.)*
WOMAN. Your sister comes and looks in on me every evening and brings me my Benson and Hedges and fixes a cup of tea. She sits, and we talk about little *Shayme*. He's a grand little fella. She's agreed you did the right thing, Brendan. How lucky was I to find you on that mountain before it was too late. I miss you terrible. Do you still listen to the classical music? Same as your father.
BRENDAN. *(Shouts to the bar.)* Dean Martin. Yes. Let's have some Dean Martin. *(He drinks the next whiskey.)* I think Dean Martin was one of the best.
WOMAN. I think Dean Martin was one of the best. I suppose you are better off not ringing so often. But write me a letter someday. It'll be something to hold, do ya see. Anyway, say a prayer every day, and I love you very much, Mammy. Write please.

Scene 15

Terrible Thing to Die Away from Home

Brendan feels in his pocket for his harmonica. Takes it out and squeezes it for fortitude. Declan the barman comes over.

DECLAN. What's that?

BRENDAN. A harmonica.

DECLAN. Terrible thing to die away from home, isn't it?

BRENDAN. It is.

DECLAN. See, that's what I mean: Some people born to annoy ya.

BRENDAN. Don't start at me.

DECLAN. That fella has looked after you like a chauffeur all these years. With your two pints Wednesday and four pints Saturday, and ne'er an emotion out of ya but that doleful half-dead look. You're like a stone, you are. "It is."

BRENDAN. *(Uncomprehending.)* I paid him.

DECLAN. I paid him. Ya harmonica prick.

BRENDAN. Fifty dollars a week. I thought it was fair. I asked him if he wanted more. I did.

DECLAN. What is your problem?

BRENDAN. That bum gave you a kick in the bolix and you deserved it, so don't start picking on me …

DECLAN. Shutup. You're just a callous shite. *(Daisy comes over. Very upset. Dressed in black.)*

DAISY. Everyone's going to the airport. Watch them put the coffin on the plane.

DECLAN. Can't open it after that, you know. They'll just stick it in the ground, and he'll never see an Irish sky again.

DAISY. He won't?

BRENDAN. His face … with the air pressure.

DAISY. Oh!

DECLAN. I'd force it open. So he could see his own sky.

DAISY. *(Crying.)* Oh!

DECLAN. Let's go.

DAISY. Are you coming, Brendan?
BRENDAN. No. I — I —
DECLAN. See, see. Some friend.
BRENDAN. I'm —
DAISY. It's okay, Brendan.
DECLAN. C'mon, Daisy. *(To Brendan.)* Shite. *(Declan and Daisy leave.)*
BRENDAN. *(Choked.)* Steveo said he was going to teach me to drive, you know. To get to work. *(Brendan holds the harmonica tighter.)*
WOMAN. It's alright, love. It's alright. I know. I know.
BRENDAN. *(Letter.)* Those early years I was drinking too much. Mammy wouldn't want to hear that — although I shouldn't be telling you either, Ashling— but it happens — kinda like solace or hide your anxiety — They're all stupid excuses. Although I could afford to do it. I'd face the dollars all the right way around in my wallet. I'd never leave them on a bar after ordering. Sign of a drunk, they'd say.

Scene 16

The Car Salesman

The used car salesman, Mike O'Leary. He is in a shiny suit.

MIKE. Good morning, sir.
BRENDAN. Hello.
MIKE. Might I interest you in …
BRENDAN. I'm just looking.
MIKE. I detect an accent.
BRENDAN. I just want to look, is all.
MIKE. There is no such thing as looking … *(Reaching out his hand.)*
WOMAN. This fella is a shyster.
BRENDAN. Brendan.
MIKE. Brendan. There is only touching and feeling, looking is for dreamers.

WOMAN. Tell him to get lost.
BRENDAN. How much are the BMWs?
WOMAN. You're some egit.
MIKE. Oh yes, yes, German engineering. How much can you spend, Brendan?
WOMAN. Never listen to me.
BRENDAN. They're probably too much for me. I just wanted —
MIKE. Ireland, right? Mike O'Leary at your service. Fifth generation. Love Ireland though. Love it. Green. Green. How long you here?
WOMAN. Look at the cheap, shiny suit, for God's sake.
BRENDAN. Five years.
MIKE. Yeah. Great-grandfather was from Kerry. You know Kerry? Or Cork. Maybe it was Cork. But great spot. Ireland, I love it there. Green. Oh yeah. Love it there. Blarney Stone. I kissed it, you know.
BRENDAN. Really
MIKE. Oh, yes. I picked it up. I looked it in the eye, and I kissed it. No procrastination. That's me, Brendan.
BRENDAN. Blarney Stone is attached to a tower.
MIKE. That's what I'm sayin'.
WOMAN. See why I have to look after you.
BRENDAN. Let me look at the cars.
MIKE. You are lookin' at the cars.
WOMAN. Give him nothing.
MIKE. BMWs
BRENDAN. I have about five to ten thousand. *(Mike puts his arm around him.)*
MIKE. Yeah, German. Not right for you. You want American. Ford. Talk tough. Talk comfort, reliability, economics, quality.
BRENDAN. Ford. Are they any good?
MIKE. Like a rock. Bob Seger. He sings it. He sings it about Ford. And whatever Bob Seger sings, I believe. You know what I'm saying. He's not putting his rep on the line unless he believes it. If he sings it, I say buy it. Oh yeah.
BRENDAN. I like this one.
WOMAN. I give up.
MIKE. Brendan. Brendan, right?
BRENDAN. Yeah.
MIKE. Seven thousand even. That's the best I can do. And let me tell you, from one Mick to another — you're making an excellent choice.

BRENDAN. Seven thousand. Okay, I'll buy it. *(Maria enters.)*
MARIA. Brendan, I'm with someone.
WOMAN. I thought we agreed on this.
MIKE. The man knows what he wants. *(They shake hands. Maria enters fully.)*
MARIA. Brendan. I'm with someone. *(Mike exits.)*

Scene 17

Looking for a Teacher

BRENDAN. I'm sorry, I'll come back.
MARIA. No. Wait there. I'll … Hide in that corner. When he goes, come back. *(He hides.)*
WOMAN. We talked about this.
BRENDAN. Will you stop talking?
WOMAN. I won't.
BRENDAN. I'm going to ask her something.
WOMAN. You better not be doing sex again.
BRENDAN. Jesus.
WOMAN. I'm warning you.
BRENDAN. What? Maybe I will do sex. Sssh.
WOMAN. Have a little respect for me. *(Maria's door opens again and Fred walks out in paint clothes.)*
FRED. That was awesome. Same time — Same bat-channel, next Tuesday. I'll finish painting your trim then.
MARIA. See ya, Fred. *(Fred exits.)*
WOMAN. And that's why his wife is looking for him.
BRENDAN. Sssssshhh
WOMAN. Ye're like calves, all coming to suckle on her teat.
MARIA. Come in. Come in. What's the matter?
BRENDAN. I want you to teach me to drive.
WOMAN. What?
MARIA. A car?
BRENDAN. Yeah.
MARIA. Have you got a car?
BRENDAN. Yeah. I just bought one. A Ford. Ford Focus. But I

can't drive it out of the lot.

WOMAN. Why don't you hire…?

MARIA. Why don't you hire an instructor?

WOMAN. Exactly.

BRENDAN. I know. But I know you. You know me. I don't know anyone else. I wouldn't be nervous with you.

MARIA. After how long here. You don't know. What about friends?

WOMAN. *(Incredulous.)* Don't talk to me.

BRENDAN. I don't really have, well, I keep to myself. I had Steveo —

WOMAN. Good looking lad like you.

MARIA. My shy Irish boy. This is a first.

BRENDAN. I can still pay you, I trust you above, I know you better than anyone.

MARIA. Expensive driving lessons, Brendan.

BRENDAN. That's okay. If I don't learn to drive I … you know, I used to get a lift every day to work. *(Pause.)* But Steveo he got killed a few days ago.

MARIA. I'm sorry to hear that, Brendan.

BRENDAN. He drove too fast.

MARIA. Well, first we have to get you a permit, and you have to pass a test. I have a friend in the registry who owes me a favor, and he can speed that up.

BRENDAN. Oh, that's great.

MARIA. And the Ford Focus? You could learn in my Saab.

BRENDAN. No, I want you to come to the dealership with me, pick it up tomorrow.

MARIA. Alright, baby.

WOMAN. Maybe your money will get you a good skill this time, at least.

BRENDAN. And I'll find a place to practice.

WOMAN. Won't give you AIDS. *(Brendan turns around. Knocks on Rose's door.)*

BRENDAN. *(Letter.)* I've started eating with a fork. Not a knife and fork. Just a fork. I say "appreciate" instead of "nice one." I say store instead of shop. "ALoominum" — instead of AlAminium. I say "What's up" instead of "What's the craic." Every day, I learn something new about America because things aren't "grand" any-more — they're "awesome." That's what happens when the rubber meets the road. And if I was to describe myself in American terms, I'd say I'm out in left field — which a lot of people think anyway — *(Standing at Rose's doorway.)*

Scene 18

Asking for Permission

Rose opens. Victor is coming behind her.

ROSE. Brendan. Hi.
VICTOR. *(Offstage.)* Hey Rose, who you talkin' to? *(Victor jumps out in the doorway.)*
ROSE. This is Victor. *(Pause.)* My brother. *(Phew.)* This is the guy I was telling you about. Gave me the chocolates.
VICTOR. *(Putting out his hand.)* Irish guy likes loud classical music. Right? *(Takes his hand away quickly before the shake can occur.)*
BRENDAN. Hi.
ROSE. Victor is one the city's finest, Brendan.
WOMAN. I think I like this girl, Brendan.
VICTOR. You got designs on my sister, Brendan?
ROSE. Shut up, Victor.
VICTOR. Hey, I'm only kidding around.
ROSE. Never mind him, Brendan.
VICTOR. I'm only saying he's got to get in line.
ROSE. You know you're an ass. I'm putting on coffee, Brendan. You want some coffee?
WOMAN. Yes, he wants coffee. He loves coffee.
BRENDAN. Okay.
ROSE. Victor was just leaving. *(Rose goes to make coffee.)*
VICTOR. You know, Brendan, I'm kinda serious too. She's a sensitive creature. Been dicked around alot. Coz of her … face. I wouldn't want you giving her the wrong idea. Gettin' her hopes up. Coz you wouldn't want to get on the wrong side of her, either.
BRENDAN. We're just friends.
VICTOR. We're all just friends.

ROSE. Goodbye, Victor! *(She pushes him off.)*
VICTOR. Call me if you need me, Rose. *(He leaves.)*
BRENDAN. I was wondering, Rose, if —
WOMAN. *(Peering in.)* Her apartment is a bit messy, isn't it?
BRENDAN. Will you shut up.
ROSE. Who me? Did you just —
BRENDAN. No, not you. I was talking —
ROSE. Yeah.
BRENDAN. It's like Tourette's. I have a form of Tourette's. Help. Shit, shit. When I get nervous. *(Woman starts laughing.)*
ROSE. That's a terrible condition.
BRENDAN. I know.
ROSE. So what did you want to ask me?
BRENDAN. I was wondering, I mean, I bought a car.
ROSE. Congratulations.
BRENDAN. Thank you, and I was wondering if you would allow me to use your parking lot to practice in.
ROSE. Practice.
BRENDAN. I have a private instructor. A friend.
ROSE. A private instructor. Are you kidding?
BRENDAN. I don't know how to drive.
ROSE. How old are you?
BRENDAN. I'm … Well …
ROSE. Never mind. It's fine. As long as the lot is clear, practice all you like.
BRENDAN. Thank you. *(Pause.)* I better go.
ROSE. You don't want the coffee, then?
BRENDAN. I don't want to disturb you any more than I did. I feel I'm intruding.
ROSE. Fine. *(She goes into her apartment.)*
WOMAN. She was expecting you to ask her out.
BRENDAN. No, she wasn't.
WOMAN. She was. She's got a big chip on her shoulder coz of her face, if that makes any sense … I think you should ask her out.
BRENDAN. I wouldn't be good enough for a woman like that.
WOMAN. That's not true. *(Maria enters in the car.)*
MARIA. You're a natural.
BRENDAN. I don't want to talk about it anymore.
WOMAN. You have to find a woman, love. Put your mother at rest. *(Brendan sits beside Maria.)*

Scene 19

First Lesson

Brendan, his head turned back. He is driving around the parking lot. Reversing.

MARIA. Now try and drive it forward.

BRENDAN. Okay. The automatic is nice.

MARIA. It sure is, buddy. Let it loose. *(Brendan begins speeding around the lot.)*

WOMAN. Oh, it's very fast.

MARIA. Now let out a shout. Yahoooooooo.

BRENDAN. Yahoo.

MARIA. Freedom — Again.

BRENDAN. YAHooooooooo

MARIA. That'a boy. How does it feel?

BRENDAN. It feels, it feels great.

MARIA. Alright, enough for tonight. You get the permit? *(He pulls the car to a stop.)*

BRENDAN. Not yet.

WOMAN. We'll get it tomorrow.

BRENDAN. I'll get it tomorrow.

MARIA. I'm arranging through my buddy for your driving test at the end of the week. *(As they get out and stand at the parked car:)*

BRENDAN. Will I be ready?

MARIA. You'll be "grand." Now tell me, have you ever been in the back seat?

BRENDAN. When I was young with my sister.

MARIA. With your sister?

BRENDAN. My father would drive

MARIA. With your sister?

BRENDAN. I liked it. Listening to Verdi and Tchaikovsky. He liked *The Nutcracker*.

MARIA. You're some fucking nutcracker. Now go down the registry tomorrow do the written test. It's logic. You'll have no problem. Pay

up all the fees and I'll sort out an appointment. Everything will be fine. *(Declan walking by. Maria slow kisses Brendan goodbye very publicly.)*
DECLAN. Get a room, Smiler.
WOMAN. Isn't that your friend Declan?
BRENDAN. *(Shaking his head.)* Why'd ya do that?
MARIA. Don't worry, Brendan, I wouldn't shame you. Just a fun kiss.
BRENDAN. *(Apologizing.)* I didn't mean —
MARIA. That's alright. I'm only a whore after all. We'll just leave it here in the lot, and I'll see you tomorrow.
BRENDAN. Maria, I wanted to say I wasn't ashamed. *(Maria looks at her watch.)*
MARIA. Yes you were. But don't worry about it. No mistake. I'm a whore. I can be your friend but I'm still a whore. This driving thing has our relationship on a different level. And sometimes I forget who I am. You know. And so that's what happened. And you reminded me. So there. *(She walks away.)* See ya tomorrow.
REGISTRY WOMAN. Says you passed.
WOMAN. Think does that Declan boy know her? You don't want this getting out, you know.

Scene 20

Registry

Brendan stands near the desk in the Registry of Motor Vehicles. He is getting his photo taken.

BRENDAN. I think I passed.
REGISTRY WOMAN. *(Wearing glasses.)* Says you did. *(Fixes his hair for the photo. It is flattened and brushed to the side. Nerd-like. He takes a photo.)*
WOMAN. Ah Brendan fix your hair nicer.
REGISTRY WOMAN. You like that one?
WOMAN. Take another.

REGISTRY WOMAN. I'll take another. *(Brendan brushes his hair to the other side.)*
BRENDAN. Do you mind?
REGISTRY WOMAN. It's fine.
WOMAN. It looks pathetic. *(Suddenly Brendan just rumples it wildly with anger.)*
BRENDAN. How's that? How's that? Is that okay?
WOMAN. There's no need to be like that.
REGISTRY WOMAN. Hey buddy, I just take the picture.
BRENDAN. *(To Registry Woman.)* I'm sorry, it's not you. Thank you. *(He takes the picture and leaves. We hear the "Barcarole" from Brendan's room.)*
WOMAN. I was just saying you always had a lovely head of hair.
BRENDAN. *(Letter.)* I got my own place after three years. Fourth floor. Got a Mastercard. Got a cactus plant. Bought a telly, TV. And then I spent eight hundred dollars on a bed. Queen size. Oh, and I bought a cookbook, too … Emeril. Anyway, you know what, Ashling, my place was, like, a cool bachelor pad.

Scene 21

Rose Stops By

Brendan's apartment — night. We hear the "Barcarole" continuing from his boom box. He looks out through the blinds in the window. There is a knock at the door.

ROSE. Hi. My turn to apologise.
BRENDAN. Come in. Come in. *(He turns off the music. The Woman is sitting in her armchair in Brendan's apartment. Rose steps in.)*
ROSE. I didn't want to disturb …
BRENDAN. No. I was just looking out the window …
ROSE. My brother …
BRENDAN. Oh yeah. He was very nice. *(She hands him some American chocolates.)*
ROSE. These are Hershey's. American.

BRENDAN. Hershey's, you didn't need … You shouldn't have …
ROSE. Stop. My brother, he's overprotective, and I was a bit quick
with you when you stopped by.
BRENDAN. No. No. You were lovely. Thank you again. The lot
is perfect. Would you like a cup of tea?
ROSE. I'm working in the morning. I should go. *(Woman stands up.)*
WOMAN. No, don't go. Don't let her go.
BRENDAN. Or whiskey.
WOMAN. *(What is he thinking and turns away.)* Oooh no, no.
ROSE. No thank you. I'll have some tea then. *(Brendan goes offstage
to make her some tea. The Woman surveys Rose closely. Rose goes and
looks out the window.)* You can see the Stop & Shop from here. It's
a good place to watch your car. *(Rose cringes at her attempt to make
conversation.)*
WOMAN. She's got lovely hair, Brendan, and a nice figure. *(Rose
starts looking through his CDs.)*
BRENDAN. *(Offstage.)* Milk, sugar?
ROSE. It's fine black or honey. If you've got honey.
WOMAN. Yanks always make it a little awkward, don't they?
BRENDAN. No honey. I can run down to the store. *(Rose admir-
ing the letter box on the table. Brendan comes out and catches her.)*
ROSE. No. No. Fine. I'm fine. *(Caught.)* That is a lovely box.
(Brendan nods okay, and he opens it.)
BRENDAN. It's just letters.
ROSE. From a girlfriend?
BRENDAN. Four letters from my mother and one from my sister.
ROSE. Oh, that is so nice. Wow. And you keep them in a box.
WOMAN. I should have written more. But I didn't even know if you
got them. Coz you never wrote back, did ya? *(Rose sits on his sofa.)*
ROSE. How often do you get to see them?
BRENDAN. Well, I haven't been home since I left, ahm, five years
ago.
ROSE. Oh, I see.
BRENDAN. *(Embarrassed.)* And we haven't written in a little while.
ROSE. Don't you call her?
WOMAN. Tell her about me. *(A car alarm goes off, and Brendan
jumps up to look out the window.)*
ROSE. It's not yours, is it?
BRENDAN. No. I just get nervous. *(Sitting beside her. Awkward.)*
ROSE. Can I ask you a question?

BRENDAN. Oh yeah.
ROSE. What do you see when you look at me?
BRENDAN. I see …
ROSE. Do you see the port-wine …
BRENDAN. Not really. I mean I know it's there but …
ROSE. How can you not see it?
BRENDAN. Because it doesn't matter I think.
ROSE. Are you making fun of me?
BRENDAN. No.
ROSE. I've never had a boyfriend. You know. Isn't that sad? *(No reply from Brendan. Awkward. Long pause.)* Listen. I'll go. I have an early start —
BRENDAN. You don't want tea?
ROSE. I'll go. *(Rose walks out.)*
BRENDAN. *(Shouts after her.)* Can I … I'll be at the Stop & Shop tomorrow. I have to get some honey and stuff.
WOMAN. What is the matter with you? Go after her. Can't you see she likes you. I don't think I can talk to you anymore. You're not the same.
BRENDAN. And why not? I'm neither here nor there. And whose fault is it?
WOMAN. Don't go blaming me. You're the one who tried to kill yourself over that Judy two-penny slut.
BRENDAN. It was a mistake. I ADMIT IT. I made a mistake.
WOMAN. *(Pause.)* I'm sorry. I'm sorry Brendan. Where are you going? *(We hear Madama Butterfly's "Humming chorus.")*

Scene 22

Fighting with Woman

Brendan sits in his car. Woman joins him, slowly. As always, sits in the back.

WOMAN. Why are we waiting in the car?
BRENDAN. Waiting for Maria.

WOMAN. Did I not take any chances, is that it? Did I protect you too much? Are you a mammy's boy? Is this my fault?
BRENDAN. I'm trying to listen to the music. Thank you.
WOMAN. If I had to go back over it, I wouldn't change a thing, you know.
BRENDAN. Too controlling.
WOMAN. Controlling. I didn't want anything to happen to you. You know you can't let Rose catch you with the prostitute. Not if you want this to work.
BRENDAN. Maria is her name. And she's my friend.
WOMAN. I know.
BRENDAN. You don't know.
WOMAN. I'm just telling you.
BRENDAN. Why can't you let me listen to my music and let me calm down?
WOMAN. Now, Brendan!
BRENDAN. Shut the hell up.
WOMAN. That's no way to talk to your mother.
BRENDAN. You're dead. You're bloody dead. *(Pause.)*
WOMAN. I only wanted to say about the prostitute —
BRENDAN. Maria. Maria.
WOMAN. You're very sensitive.
BRENDAN. And who made me that way?
WOMAN. Now, Brendan. Lets not start again. I brought you up as good and safe as possible.
BRENDAN. Like a feckin' Molly. Tied to your apron strings, like a baby suckling on the tit too long.
WOMAN. I protected you.
BRENDAN. Yeah, and see where that got ya. Forcing me away from my own home. Telling me not to come home. Even for your funeral. Makin' sure Ashling doesn't write until you're in the grave. I'm not an egit, you know.
WOMAN. Well, I'm not leaving. *(Maria approaches and gets in the car.)*
MARIA. Did I hear you shouting at somebody?
WOMAN. You certainly did.
BRENDAN. No.
MARIA. So you're driving on the road tonight.
BRENDAN. Ah, I don't know.
MARIA. Let's go. Start her up. Signal left. And pull out. *(He starts*

it up. He turns out on the road and a horn beeps. A shout: "What are you doing?" He freezes.) Go. Go. Keep going.
BRENDAN. God — *(Lights of another car, coming against them. More horns.)*
MARIA. Brake. God. Brake. *(He brakes suddenly, and Maria is thrown forward.)* Damn. You're starting to make my day job look damn easy.
WOMAN. What did I tell you about cars, Brendan? Hah. *(Maria rubs Brendan's neck.)*
MARIA. You're alright. Take off smoothly.
WOMAN. You know, you're just angry at me, but it's your fault too. You're afraid to be happy. You need a proper woman. *(There are more beeping horns. Brendan is starting to lose his cool. He jumps out of the car. In the middle of the road.)*
MARIA. Brendan, where are you going? Get back in the car. *(Brendan gets in a fighting stance. Fists out.)*
BRENDAN. Fuck off the lot of ye. Fuck off. C'mon. C'mon. I'll take you all on. C'mon. Ya Ya. Ya ya. C'mon.
MARIA. *(Shouting out the window.)* Brendan, get in the car.
WOMAN. You're making a fool of yourself. People are looking at ya.
BRENDAN. I don't care if ye are looking at me. C'mon on. *(He stands with his fists out. Waiting to take on the world. Maria comes to him.)*
MARIA. Okay. C'mon, Brendan. I'll drive. *(He calms with her touch. She escorts him to the passenger side. Cars still beeping. She grabs her breasts to tell the traffic what they can do with themselves. Maria gets in the driver's side herself.)*
WOMAN. What is the matter with you? *(Maria reverses the car back into the lot.)*
MARIA. Are you alright?
BRENDAN. Yeah.
MARIA. You sure. *(Pause.)* I'll let you cool off. *(She leaves. Brendan gets out in the parking lot and walks away too.)*
WOMAN. Mammy died last week, and we buried her three days ago. She wouldn't let me tell you until after she was buried and that was her way. You know yourself.
BRENDAN. Jesus Christ. *(He goes.)*

Scene 23

Griffin's Pub to Ease Stress

Brendan is in a corner in Griffin's, drinking. The Woman is beside him.

WOMAN. Like your father. Find solace in the bottom of a glass.

BRENDAN. No peace anywhere now, hah?

WOMAN. You're not yourself.

BRENDAN. I am myself. You're driving me mad.

WOMAN. You have to let go. Mourn and then go on.

BRENDAN. *(Imitating snidely.)* "Mourn and then go on."

WOMAN. At least you're talking to me. Even if it's like a baby. *(Declan walks in. Declan is drunk.)*

DECLAN. Oh, look in the corner. Bolix himself. *(Brendan ignoring him.)* Not talking, Brendan? Are ya feeling bad over here, all alone?

BRENDAN. Yeah.

DECLAN. You don't show your last respects at the airport. Them are your colours. Loyal to those who you can get something off. You know what they call that, boys? A bloody parasite.

WOMAN. I'm proud of you, Brendan. Coming over here. Making it by yourself.

DECLAN. You know who I saw him with the other night. A dirty wraparound.

DECLAN. Pallin' with whores is all your type is good for. People who sell themselves for money. Parasites and whores all the same.

BRENDAN. *(Shouts.)* What have I done to you? *(Brendan stands up in fight mode.)*

WOMAN. Sit down, Brendan.

BRENDAN. Too long sitting down. C'mon —

DECLAN. Apart from your lack of respect of Steveo. I don't like you. Your family shoved you off coz you're an embarrassment. Coz you're weak. You look weak. *(Fred walks up.)* You remind me of those helpless fellas on the street with an empty bottle rolled beside them.

41

Can't stand for anything. Just fuckin' losers. *(Declan reaches over the bar and gets a bottle of pills. He throws them at Brendan.)* Here's some more Tylenol. You should finish the job this time. *(Brendan is motionless. Frozen by the volley. Lost. Fred steps in between them.)*
FRED. Declan. Okay.
DECLAN. Glad you're becoming a Yank — they can keep ya. You're no more Irish now than a stream of piss.
FRED. Enough. Get out, Declan. *(Declan walks away.)* Brendan don't pay him no attention. He's drunk. Upset about Steveo. *(Brendan sits. Fred sits with him.)*
WOMAN. That is a miserable young man. Malignant to the core.
FRED. It was uncalled for, Brendan.
BRENDAN. Yeah.
FRED. What did he mean by the Tylenol?
BRENDAN. Nothing. I'll have my license next week, you know. I can drive to work.
FRED. Great, great. I was meaning to say … something I wanted to talk to you about, Brendan. Am, at the moment, I just haven't got a position for you. With Steveo gone and yourself. Well, I've decided to cut back a bit, you know. To a smaller crew.
BRENDAN. I've been with you a good while.
FRED. I know. I'm not saying this is easy. It's not. If I had something you're the first man on the totem pole. Consolidation. It's part of the business.
BRENDAN. Is this coz of telling your wife you were gone?
FRED. No. No. I just decided. It's about less overhead, more profit.
BRENDAN. I don't want to work with anyone else. I'm comfortable.
FRED. I have no choice.
BRENDAN. I started before anyone else on your crew.
FRED. Maybe it's time you had a change. Travel the country, see things. *(Beat.)* Was Declan right? He see you with a prostitute?
BRENDAN. You mean Maria?
FRED. Is that her name?
BRENDAN. Yeah. She's a friend.
FRED. Right. *(Woman moves off.)*
BRENDAN. You know who she is. Lives on Pine Street.
FRED. No. No. *(We hear the low strains of* Carmina Burana. *But never more than low and mixed with street noises. The Woman starts reciting the letters to him again.)*
WOMAN. Hello, Brendan. You are gone three years and I'm pining.

FRED. Am, can I buy you a drink?
WOMAN. Brendan, this is my third letter to you. My heart is in turmoil and I made you go.
BRENDAN. Keep your drink. *(Brendan gets up and leaves.)*

Scene 24

The Mirror

Brendan walks back towards the apartment. The Woman beside him. His car in the background. A hooded kid hovers, pedestrians cross.

WOMAN. You are better off away from here and not to be leading your life around me. I lived a good life, Brendan, and I know we saw sadness when your father died.
BRENDAN. There ya go again. Maudlin shit. With your "oh God help us" and "I live a good life" and bloody "woe is me" guilt.
WOMAN. You and Ashling were my support, and there's nothing I wouldn't do for you
BRENDAN. Go.
WOMAN. It broke my heart to see you go.
BRENDAN. You. You should go. You.
WOMAN. But I was proud you were going to make something of yourself. Get away from the town. So don't blame me or feel bad. Even though I know some say it was a disgrace a mother pushing her son out the door like that. It was for your own good.
BRENDAN. Bolix, I shamed ya
WOMAN. You are such a soft, kind-hearted boy. Don't come back, or it would be even harder to leave.
BRENDAN. Don't come back, or it would be even harder to leave. What kind of love is that? What kind of love is that? Answer me. What?
WOMAN. Anyway, say a prayer every day, and I love you very much. Mammy. Write please. *(A hooded kid is kicking the side of the car. Then breaks the side mirror off it. Just being brazen out of bore-*

dom. Wrong car at the wrong time.)
BRENDAN.   Hey. Hey. Hey. That's my car. *(Carmina Burana loudens. Brendan catches the kid. Brendan attacks him — a catharsis of anger. He punches him in the face. The kid punches back. Brendan lays into him. People walking by, shout — One gets on his cellphone — They form a semi-circle. The kid falls, broken. The music fades out. We hear sirens. Brendan stops. What has he done? The kid is on the ground. Motionless. The Bum breaks through the circle. Brendan falls off to the side.)*
BUM. Is he dead? *(Victor the cop appears. He starts taking names.)*

Scene 25

Jail

A bloodied Brendan is sitting. The Woman is beside him, watching him. It is jail.

BRENDAN.   *(Letter.)* Ashling, they put you in jail over here if you're drunk on the street. To protect you from anything happening to you. It's a good idea isn't it. But I was thinking if they did that in Ireland everyone would be in jail. I'm not supposed to say that, am I? Anyway — *(Victor comes in in full regalia.)*
VICTOR. How ya like life behind bars, Brendan? *(Brendan stands. Goes to him.)*
BRENDAN. Victor, is the boy bad?
VICTOR. He's on life support.
BRENDAN. I don't know …
VICTOR. Heard he scratched your car? Did you see him?
BRENDAN. He was breaking the mirror. Broke it off the side. It doesn't matter.
VICTOR. The kid was a screw-up, delinquent. He was pulled in twice for breaking and entering. One was an elderly couple, wife ended up in hospital, minor heart attack after stumbling on him.
BRENDAN. It was just a mirror.
WOMAN. I'll say a prayer for him.

BRENDAN. What's going to happen?
VICTOR. Haul you in front of a judge, you plead and, depending on that, you get bail, or jail. Good lawyer will say you were defending your property, which you were … So, Rose likes you. I know she is dying to get married, kids. You ready for that, Brendan?
BRENDAN. *(Still stunned by the boy.)* I didn't think about …
VICTOR. Are you going to ask her out, is what I'm asking you?
BRENDAN. I think I've killed someone …
VICTOR. But would you?
BRENDAN. And you want to know if I'll ask your sister out.
VICTOR. Would you ask her out, is what I'm asking?
BRENDAN. Yes. I don't know. Of course I would. Are you trying to drive me mad? Why are …
VICTOR. Ahh, but being behind bars makes you see time is precious. It fuels your regrets, the things you should have done. Life passes by and you get left behind. You know.
BRENDAN. Victor, at this moment I'm worried if 've I killed the poor boy? *(Victor double-taking and enjoying his malice.)*
VICTOR. The kid is alright. Broke his arm, couple of scratches. I was kidding. Wanted to see your face. *(He laughs.)*
BRENDAN. Jesus.
VICTOR. And that was a hell of a face. *(Victor nods yes.)*
BRENDAN. That wasn't funny.
VICTOR. Hey, you deserved the fright. You ain't supposed to be going around beating the hell out of people. *(Pause. Brendan tries to compose himself.)* Okay. You can go. Remember what I said about Rose. She likes you. Just be back tomorrow at eight A.M. for arraignment. You're in my good books, kid. Coz I like your a, a, a, pugnaciousness. Yeah. *(We hear Victor's dirty laugh as he walks off. Brendan walks out, with the Woman behind him.)*
WOMAN. Now that is the epitome of a dirty-lookin' tinker. And if I say it, I will, a shit. There. I said it. A shit. *(We see people lined up at a T stop. They are those other characters, in various pedestrian disguises, not in the scene.)*
BRENDAN. They could end up taking the citizenship away from me because of this.
WOMAN. No.

Scene 26

Daisy Goes Home

Brendan sees Daisy coming down the other side of the street as he walks out. She is wheeling a large suitcase. It topples a little, her coat falls off it.

DAISY. Ah shoot. Hi, Brendan.

BRENDAN. Hi, Daisy.

DAISY. What happened your face?

BRENDAN. Oh nothing. I fell — Where are you going?

DAISY. Home.

BRENDAN. Home where?

DAISY. Where the hell do ya think. Where's home?

BRENDAN. Ireland?

DAISY. Yeah.

BRENDAN. Oh. Are you going now?

DAISY. No. I'm just practicing rolling my fuckin' suitcase down the street.

BRENDAN. Is everything alright?

DAISY. Everything is fine.

BRENDAN. Do you want a hand?

DAISY. No. *(We hear a train coming from behind her.)* That's my train coming. *(He picks up her suitcase.)*

BRENDAN. I'll help you. When are you coming back?

DAISY. I don't know. I'm sick of this place. I'm sick of the struggle. I don't know anyone. I know people. I don't really know them like I know them at home. America is lonely. *(Reaching the train stop.)*

BRENDAN. I suppose.

DAISY. You know. There's a lot of people here and you're lonely, that's not right, you know.

BRENDAN. Have you a place to stay?

DAISY. Yeah. Back in with my mortified mother. How do you like that?

BRENDAN. It's safer, isn't it. Sometimes it's scary over here.

DAISY. (*Last desperation bid.*) Would ya look after me? Is that what you mean?
BRENDAN. Well —
WOMAN. Brendan, no.
DAISY. You're a good man, Brendan. Everyone needs a good man. (*Brendan is blank, and Daisy realises her desperation.*) I'm making a fool of myself still, amn't I? Yeah. That's why I better go. I'm pregnant Brendan. Steveo. "Feck sake." (*Smiles.*)
BRENDAN. Ooh.
DAISY. You didn't know? I thought everyone knew. I was the talk of the town.
BRENDAN. It doesn't matter does it?
WOMAN. Stop giving her ideas.
BRENDAN. Why don't you stay?
WOMAN. The last thing you need is a feckin' baby.
DAISY. No. I'm going. I didn't mean to be mean earlier, you know. You should see a doctor about that bruise.
BRENDAN. It's okay.
DAISY. Can I contact you? Can I write you, like?
BRENDAN. Oh yeah. Yeah, please. You have my address? (*The train arrives, and the doors open. Daisy is getting on.*)
DAISY. I do. (*She stops after Brendan lifts her bags on, and she steps off. She kisses Brendan quickly and lovely. She steps back on, and the doors close. Daisy leaves.*)
WOMAN. You know you were early too, ya know.
BRENDAN. What?
WOMAN. Ah ya know, your father and me was in love, too, but sometimes ya can't wait. We did it on the beach.
BRENDAN. Shut up, for God's sake.
WOMAN. I got sand everywhere. We were going to call ya Sandy as a joke. But we called you Brendan instead, after his father. Brendan is a nice name though.
BRENDAN. (*Letter.*) I know you're wondering, Ashling, if I found, as Mammy said, "a nice American girl" yet. But sure you know me. I'm too shy. But the American girls are lovely. I think sometimes when one talks to me at a bar that she's beautiful, and I'd like to tell her, but that would sound stupid. I mean, she'd probably think I'm a freak. So, I just don't say anything, and then they walk away thinking I am a freak.

Scene 27

Asking Rose

Brendan starts looking at the car. He stands emotionless and then moves his finger along a scratch. He is trying to tape up the mirror. Woman watching him. Rose walks up.

ROSE. How did your driving lesson go? *(Brendan looks up. A little astonished. She goes to look at the car.)* This is the new car. Ahh, Brendan. I'm sorry. What happened your face? That's just not right.
BRENDAN. It's okay —
ROSE. We have to do something. I'll call my brother.
BRENDAN. He knows. I was in jail last night for fighting with the kid who broke it. That's how my face — I got angry over a mirror. I was stupid.
ROSE. I'd kill anyone if they touched my car.
BRENDAN. The kid is alright though. Thank God. Your brother was very helpful.
ROSE. Do you have to go to court?
BRENDAN. Tomorrow. Are you going to work now? Can I walk you in? *(Rose is surprised at his awkward proposal.)*
ROSE. If you like. *(Walking together.)*
BRENDAN. Do you know how to drive?
ROSE. Since I was sixteen.
BRENDAN. When I pass my test. I want to drive to the Metropolitan Opera House in New York and park outside and go in with my ticket and listen.
ROSE. To what?
BRENDAN. To something with … You know.
ROSE. Passion.
BRENDAN. Yeah.
ROSE. I'm never been to the opera.
BRENDAN. Neither have I but the idea sounds … impressive. *(He smiles.)* Doesn't it?
ROSE. There's that smile of yours, are you trying to impress me?

(Brendan gets embarrassed.) I'm only joking. Jesus, you're very shy. *(At the store.)* Well, here we are. I have to go in.
WOMAN. Ask her
BRENDAN. OK. I'll seeya. *(Pause.)* Can I ask you, if you like, I mean don't feel obliged, I mean, I don't ask, I'm not used to asking anyone or people or girls, I mean, you know. I just wondered because …
ROSE. I have to go in Brendan.
WOMAN. *(Impatient.)* Ask her.
BRENDAN. I'm sorry. You think I'm an idiot, I'm not able to express, I can't say, I mean, I'm going to become a citizen on Friday and my friend, I was going to ask my friend Steveo to come with me.
WOMAN. *(Exasperated.)* Jesus.
BRENDAN. And he can't now, you know, and I was wondering if you would accompany me. That's so old-fashioned. As a friend, in a way, you know, like —
ROSE. Are you asking me out?
BRENDAN. I wanted …
ROSE. To your citizenship?
BRENDAN. It's this Friday at twelve.
ROSE. I'd love to go. I just have to check my schedule.
BRENDAN. You don't have to feel forced or
ROSE. No. So you were trying to impress me fighting on the street, opera, and citizenship ceremony. A real man. *(She gives him a kiss. He is transfixed with her.)* You know, we kinda look alike now. Seeya later.
WOMAN. Oh, Thank You, God. *(Brendan smiles at Woman.)*
BRENDAN. *(Breathes heavily.)* That wasn't too hard.
WOMAN. Now, you just have to throw on some of that Irish charm of yours for the judge.
BRENDAN. How long more are you sticking around?
WOMAN. Until … *(Maria joins them.)*
BRENDAN. Until what.
WOMAN. Am I annoying you? *(Woman laughs.)*
BRENDAN. *(Letter.)* I know Mammy would be at ya and all while telling you it was for your own good. I used to play the harmonica off key just to annoy her back, but she'd talk right through it as if it didn't bother her at all. Ashling, it was one thing to leave home and know you mightened see Mammy again. But it's another thing knowing you'll never see her again. You know.

Scene 28

Driving Lesson with a Treat

Brendan sits in the car with the Woman as Maria joins them.

MARIA. What happened to your face?
BRENDAN. I beat myself up.
MARIA. What the hell happened to the mirror?
BRENDAN. About, about last night. The scene I made — shouting at the cars. *(Smiles.)* Foolish.
MARIA. Don't mention it. No need.
BRENDAN. Sorry about it.
MARIA. We all have to let off steam. Right? I just do it in the bed with the S and M's. Give them an extra whipping. Lash the ass off them. And walk across their back in my stilettos. They love it.
WOMAN. Imagine me walking across your father's back in my stilettos. *(Brendan takes the car out of the lot. Same place as the previous night, but this time much more secure.)*
MARIA. C'mon. Born to be wild, Brendan. Drive it, baby. *(Brendan using turn signals. Driving. A car blows past them.)* Ohh. Shout at the taxi. Shout at him. Dickhead. Say "Dickhead." *(Brendan rolls down the window.)*
BRENDAN. *(Shouts.)* Dickhead. Yeah, you. *(Maria starts laughing.)*
WOMAN. Very mature.
MARIA. Drive her Brendan. Yeehaaaa!
WOMAN. Maybe your father should have got a few lessons in the bed like you. Hah? Would have done him good.
MARIA. Well, I think you're ready. I think we should celebrate.
BRENDAN. Right. What had you in mind?
WOMAN. It's almost liberating, watching the way Maria goes about what she does. You know, I spent my life worrying what others would think. *(Maria starts to play with his fly)*
MARIA. Consider it a freebie.
BRENDAN. A freebie.
WOMAN. Now, Brendan, you are a man of substance.

BRENDAN. Here?
MARIA. *(Smiling with devilishness.)* Where else?
WOMAN. Rose —
BRENDAN. In the lot?
WOMAN. For God's sake, Rose.
BRENDAN. *(Stopping her.)* There's someone …
MARIA. What? Someone else. Brendan.
BRENDAN. Yeah.
MARIA. I'm jealous. She's nice?
BRENDAN. She is nice.
WOMAN. All these years, just you and me, and then you …
BRENDAN. Well it wasn't just you and me.
MARIA. *(Feigning shock.)* What do you mean?
BRENDAN. Well, you had other, others — Oh, I didn't mean anything. I just like someone … The first time … For …
MARIA. Are you dumping me?
BRENDAN. No.
MARIA. Ahh, I'm just bustin' your chops. I'm glad for you. Who is she?
BRENDAN. Rose. *(We hear the low strains of "La donna e mobile.")*
MARIA. That's her name? Like the chocolates you gave me once.
BRENDAN. Yeah.
MARIA. I'll check her out and give you the thumbs up if I like her. Anyway, I'll see you tomorrow morning. Eleven A.M. is the test. I'll be outside your apartment waiting for you.
BRENDAN. Thanks, Maria. Thank you.

Scene 29

Last Letter from Home

Woman is sitting on her chair. Music is heard. Brendan dances with his clothes as he prepares to put them on.

WOMAN. Hello, Brendan. You're five years gone now, and I still mark the date you left on the calendar. I'm not in the best healthwise at the minute. The lungs feel heavy and I know, I know you are cursing them cigarettes, but it is my only outlet now. Brendan, I know I told you before you left not to come back for my funeral, and I'm right. Don't be alarmed now, I'm not dying, but I would just want to tell you to keep getting on with your life. *(He mouths in a hearty exaggerated manner the words [which he doesn't know] of the aria — while conducting with the iron — and pressing his shirt. He puts on the shirt and pants. He admires himself.)* You wouldn't believe how much this country has changed since you've been gone. It reminds me of America, even though I've never been there. It just seems very fast now. Brendan, I sometimes think you are forgetting me. Don't forget me, love, there isn't a day goes by when I don't think about you and wish you were here. Have you found a nice American girl or something? I hope so, I'd like to think you were in the arms of someone you love. Anyway, say a prayer every day, and I love you very much. Mammy. Write please. *(There is a knock at the door. It is Rose. He answers it. She steps in the doorway.)*

BRENDAN. *(Embarrassed.)* Hi, Rose. Come in.

ROSE. I thought I heard music —

BRENDAN. *(He turns off the music.)* Too loud again. I'll never learn.

ROSE. It's that passion we talked about, I guess.

BRENDAN. Yeah.

WOMAN. Hard to contain it all, right?

BRENDAN. I was just trying on my clothes for tomorrow.

ROSE. You look good.

BRENDAN. You think so?

ROSE. I got you something. *(She hands him an envelope.)*

BRENDAN. *(Shocked by the thought.)* That's ... I ... You shouldn't have done ... I didn't expect ...

ROSE. *(Hands a box to him.)* Open the damn thing. *(He opens it gently.)* Oh, come on, rip it off.

BRENDAN. I'll open it slowly so I can enjoy the surprise.

WOMAN. Maybe I did Molly you.

ROSE. It's just a gift.

BRENDAN. Two tickets to, the opera, *Il Trovatore.*

ROSE. This guy Verdi wrote it, they said. I know it's not the Met. It's our local one.

BRENDAN. Oh, no, this is brilliant. Yes. Thank you.

ROSE. You seem — not so excited.

WOMAN. You should be over the moon.

BRENDAN. I just get sad inside, that's all.
ROSE. How can you be sad? It's a good thing.
BRENDAN. I don't know how to handle it.
ROSE. Oh, come on.
BRENDAN. *(Newly excited.)* You know, that's what I was listening to the night you asked me to turn down the music.
ROSE. Really.
BRENDAN. Yeah.
ROSE. What do you know. I'm good.
BRENDAN. *(More excited.)* Hey, will you come with me?
ROSE. Who do you think the other ticket is for? *(Pause.)* Okay. I like you, Brendan, I do. I was attracted to you when I saw you and, God, I wouldn't have said this years ago. So I'm just saying that I like you. I trust you. I want to trust you. You know what I mean?
BRENDAN. I trust you too, like as well.
ROSE. And I'm glad you asked me to your ceremony. I think it's an honor.
WOMAN. Tell her about me, Brendan.
BRENDAN. I want to tell you something. Why I haven't got a letter in a while from my mother. You asked the other night.
ROSE. The box of letters. Yeah. Don't you call her?
BRENDAN. Well, she's not alive now.
ROSE. Oh, I'm sorry. When did she pass on?
WOMAN. Last week.
BRENDAN. Last week. *(Short pause.)*
ROSE. Last week — You didn't go home for the funeral?
BRENDAN. Well it … no … it. I —
ROSE. I'm sorry, I'm sorry, I shouldn't have asked that. *(Brendan begins to fight back his tears. Rose comes over to him. She gives him a big hug.)* I'm sorry. *(He hugs her back. And then slowly begins to cry. He wipes his face on his shirt. But now, he can't stop. He pulls away from her. Face in the shirt. An uncontrollable crying. A release. He gathers himself. He stands to shake it off.)*
BRENDAN. I'm fine. I'm just a little — I'm just a little upset. Sometimes we didn't get on — you know, and other times we did, and I didn't see her for a long time — you know, and now she's gone, and I can only think back — look back and remember— you know. And it kinda hurts, you know. — I ruined my shirt. *(She hugs him again, tighter.)*
ROSE. It's alright. *(He walks away a little.)*

BRENDAN. I don't like you to see me like this.

ROSE. Why not? Worse if there was nobody to see you.

BRENDAN. Yeah.

ROSE. Would you like me to stay?

BRENDAN. Okay. (*Rose takes him by the hand, and they sit. She kisses him, softly. He touches her face. They hold hands. They look out.*)

ROSE. This is nice, isn't it?

BRENDAN. It is. (*We enjoy the moment.*)

Scene 30

Court

COURT OFFICER. All rise. May it please the court in the case of Suffolk County versus Brendan Roche. Reading of charges, misdemeanor, assault, and battery against Michael Antonio Galliano — Case number 57624587B976. Court is now in session. The honorable Philip J. Casey presiding. (*Rose helps Brendan put on a tie as we hear the court officer. Rose leaves. Judge enters. A court officer beside him. Brendan enters. Women stands.*)

JUDGE. Have we met before, Mr. Roche?

BRENDAN. No, sir, your honour.

WOMAN. That's the man's house you painted. Don't lie.

JUDGE. You're up for citizenship, I see.

BRENDAN. Yes, sir, your honour.

JUDGE. Some fine citizen duties you performed, then.

WOMAN. He recognises you. He knows you're lying. Will you listen to me?

JUDGE. You think, Mr. Roche, they will allow you to become a citizen with an assault and battery charge on your record.

WOMAN. Tell him you remember him.

BRENDAN. Your honor, I made a mistake. But I'm very proud to be living here, and to have the chance to become a citizen means a lot to me.

JUDGE. Why should I believe you, Mr. Roche?

WOMAN. Oh, God.

BRENDAN. Because it's the truth, sir. Your honour.

JUDGE. The truth. And you don't lie, do you, Mr. Roche?
WOMAN. Ahh, shit.
BRENDAN. Your honour, whatever punishment you give me, it's nothing compared to taking that chance away from me.
JUDGE. You took that away from yourself, Mr. Roche. *(Pause.)* I can't endorse violence by letting it happen because we feel we have the law on our side. In this case, it obviously seemed excessive. You do say you're sorry, and I've lost enough mirrors to understand your action … but it's still against the law. That said, I choose not to make a note of this in your record, you caught me on a good day, Mr. Roche. I'm all patriotic. You will, however, do fifty hours of community service.
BRENDAN. Thank you, your honour.
JUDGE. I will tell you one other thing, Mr. Roche. Call it a mitigating response. You're lucky my wife was very pleased with the painting work you did. *(Maria is sitting on the steps outside his apartment building.)*
WOMAN. Well, if that isn't the luck of the Irish.
MARIA. Brendan.

Scene 31

Maria Waiting for Him

MARIA. I've been waiting for you.
BRENDAN. I'm sorry I'm late.
MARIA. We got to get going. *(Rose and Victor come out the main door.)*
ROSE. Brendan.
VICTOR. Well, hello there, Maria. *(Maria turns around. Surprised. Brendan realizes they might know each other, and he stops.)*
MARIA. Victor.
VICTOR. What are you doing here?
ROSE. She's a friend of Brendan's. Right? She's teaching you to drive?
BRENDAN. This is uh, Rose.
MARIA. Rose!
VICTOR. Driving instructor? Is that what he calls you?

WOMAN. Oh, I'm wishing the ground would swallow you up.
MARIA. I'm his friend, that's right, and I'm also teaching Brendan to drive.
VICTOR. You going legit, Maria?
ROSE. Is everything okay?
BRENDAN. The judge gave me some community service. But I better get going —
VICTOR. Going for a drive now, Brendan?
WOMAN. Brendan, go, for God's sake.
ROSE. *(To Victor.)* How do you know each other?
VICTOR. I've locked our Maria up a few times.
ROSE. For what?
MARIA. Prostitution, darling. Whoring myself. Great job, but the hours can be hell.
BRENDAN. Hey
MARIA. I'm sorry Brendan. But this friggin' guy.
ROSE. Are you two … Oh my God. Jesus Christ. What was I supposed to be Brendan. The bit on the side. What was this all … Who do you think …
MARIA. Hey, don't be getting all twisted, girl. Brendan is just my friend. Told me he liked you. That you and him, That you were friends. Maybe more
ROSE. More what, a disease maybe.
MARIA. I'm cleaner than you, darlin'.
VICTOR. Watch your …
ROSE. Shut up Victor. *(To Maria.)* Do you sit around and laugh at how he was making a fool of me?
BRENDAN. No. That's not right, Rose. Maria is my friend. That's the truth.
ROSE. Anything else.
BRENDAN. She is someone I respect and has been awful good to me …
ROSE. How good?
BRENDAN. Good.
ROSE. How good?
BRENDAN. Maria was there when there was no one to talk to.
ROSE. And now I'm there. Yeah.
BRENDAN. No.
ROSE. Do you pay her for sex?
WOMAN. Oh no.

ROSE. Do you pay her for sex?
MARIA. We don't have to …
ROSE. Do you pay her for sex?
BRENDAN. Yes, I did. But …
WOMAN. Ooh!
ROSE. That's all I needed to know.
BRENDAN. But not since I met you.
ROSE. Well, whoopee-dee-doo. Why don't you just give me fifty bucks and we'll call it quits.
BRENDAN. Rose, I told Maria about you. I told her about you, and I haven't felt like this for someone in a long, in a long time, I haven't felt anything … and you I want to go with —
ROSE. We're going nowhere, Irish boy. *(Rose turns defiantly and walks off.)*
VICTOR. I told you not to dick her around, Brendan. Didn't I? And then you pull this stunt — buddy. I should have left you in jail. You're no better than that thug kid you beat up. *(Victor walks off.)*
MARIA. Hey Victor, you should come over sometime — my treat. *(We begin to hear the "Humming Chorus." The state cop enters, sits in the passenger side. He is in all his fine regalia, an imposing force.)*
WOMAN. Well, that's one for the folks back home, isn't it? *(Woman gets in the back seat.)*
MARIA. C'mon Brendan, we're late for the test. *(Brendan sits beside the State Cop.)*

Scene 32

The Driving Test

The "Humming Chorus" continues to play. Brendan is near the end of his test. The Statey looking severe. Concentrating on Brendan while ticking off boxes on his sheet, haphazard. He draws out the tension by watching a nervous Brendan, intently.

STATE COP. So if you listen to the music, you're able to drive. Right?

BRENDAN. Yeah. Keeps me steady.
STATE COP. I hate this music.
BRENDAN. Oh!
STATE COP. *(Looking at him intently, and then:)* You passed.
BRENDAN. *(Excited.)* I passed. I passed.
MARIA. Well. *(Maria enters and lets out a shriek of excitement as Brendan tells her.)*
BRENDAN. I passed.
STATE COP. I've got a bit of business to take care of.
MARIA. Thanks, Jim.
BRENDAN. Thank you. Thank you, Maria. Thank you for everything.
MARIA. That's my pleasure. I'm sorry about this morning.
BRENDAN. Ahhh.
MARIA. Hey, if she ain't able to see your kindness and forgive you no matter what — you know.
BRENDAN. Nothing to forgive. You're my friend. *(Maria kisses him, friendly. They hug. Brendan is proud.)*
MARIA. Look at the mirror. I'd a kicked his head in, too. So, where next?
BRENDAN. I've got no work scheduled, as such. I might visit the ol' sod.
MARIA. Say hello to your mother and all that?
BRENDAN. Yeah. I suppose.
WOMAN. Ask her if she'd like to go?
BRENDAN. Would you like to go?
WOMAN. I was kidding.
MARIA. I can't, darling. I'm booked up for the week.
WOMAN. Imagine their faces in town, this one on your arm.
BRENDAN. I didn't mean. I meant, you know, as a friend.
MARIA. I know, darling.
WOMAN. I like her. I do, Brendan.
BRENDAN. But, I'm going to the opera, first.
MARIA. The opera.
BRENDAN. Might go to Memphis, too. See Elvis' grave, and I'd like to see the Black Hills of Dakota and Mount Rushmore.
MARIA. And Vegas while you're at it.
BRENDAN. Yeah.
MARIA. Well, I better get going.
BRENDAN. You want a lift?

MARIA. No, Jim is giving me a lift. *(We see Jim, the Statey, waiting at the side. He gives a nod.)* How'd you think I got you fixed up so quickly?
BRENDAN. I owe you money.
MARIA. That's okay. Just put it down to kindred spirits. I left you a little present in the car. See ya. *(She leaves. He takes the present out of the passenger side. It has a ribbon on it.)*
WOMAN. Is that the present?
BRENDAN. A hip-hop CD. Says "Put it to good use, Love Maria."
WOMAN. You'll find the right one yet.
BRENDAN. I found the right one.

Scene 33

Love in the Doorway

Brendan is at Rose's door. He knocks.

WOMAN. Now remember, from the letter I wrote you, recite this: I just wanted to say —
BRENDAN. I just wanted to say —
WOMAN. We all do the best we can —
BRENDAN. We all do the best we can — *(Rose opens it.)*
ROSE. I'm not going to the opera, Brendan.
BRENDAN. I just wanted to say —
ROSE. I'm not going.
BRENDAN. Do you want the tickets back?
ROSE. No, keep them.
BRENDAN. If you change your mind —
ROSE. I mean, you think you know someone.
WOMAN. Now. Now.
BRENDAN. I just wanted to say we all do the best we can. We make friends when we can make friends, and we love even when we can't help it. Some people are lonely and some people are happy, but we're all the same and as long as we are good, just a good person then we're alright, and, and Maria is a good person.

ROSE. I'm sure she is. It just makes me feel like an idiot.
BRENDAN. Why?
ROSE. Why? Why? Because I LIKE you.
BRENDAN. I like you too.
ROSE. Well, she can have ya.
BRENDAN. Ah, Rose.
ROSE. What, what do you expect me to say?
BRENDAN. That you want to go to the opera with me.
ROSE. No.
BRENDAN. I'll leave the tickets under your door. Maybe.
ROSE. How do I know you won't be visiting her?
BRENDAN. I will be visiting her.
ROSE. See, see.
BRENDAN. As a friend. Only as a friend.
ROSE. No.
BRENDAN. *(Pause.)* Speaking personally, like, Rose, it's hard to
be alone. *(We hear Pachelbel's "Canon and Gigue" in D major.)*
ROSE. I'm not alone. *(She walks back in and closes the door.)*
WOMAN. She's pretty stubborn, isn't she.

Scene 34

The Letter to Ashling

We hear the music, and we watch him finish off his letter.

BRENDAN. *(Letter.)* Well, Ashling, I'll finish up — I know this
letter is a bit late, five years or so, but it took me a long time to
write it. You know me. I know I only rang once, but I was always
thinking about you, Mammy, Shayme and Maurice. *(He gets his
jacket. Puts the letter in an envelope. Seals it.)*
WOMAN. *(In sync with Brendan from "You know me" and continuing to recite the rest of the letter by herself after "Maurice.")* You
know me. I know I only rang once, but I was always thinking
about you, Mammy, Shayme and Maurice. I went and I never
looked back, as Mammy said to me. I miss you all, and I missed

the funeral, but I know that was meant to be. And don't feel bad because them were Mammy's wishes. She'd torment you until you gave in to her. Wouldn't she? I talk to her every day, you know.
BRENDAN. *(To Woman.)* Are you coming with me? Come on.
WOMAN. No. I don't want to.
BRENDAN. Will you be here when I get back?
WOMAN. I might. Fix your hair, love. Okay. *(He looks at her and smiles. He knows. He fixes it and goes to the car. He gets in the car. He takes off.)* I bought a car, Ashling, and I'm driving now. I passed the test. I should have learnt years ago, but you have to be able to drive in America, otherwise you're lost. It is a Ford Focus. Big blue one. If we were all together, we'd go for a drive. We'd go to New York, and I'd bring you to the opera house. I was going to bring a girlfriend, Rose. I finally found a "nice American girl." She is beautiful. But she backed out at the last minute for personal reasons. *(A car cuts him off. He beeps the horn.)*
BRENDAN. What the, buddy. Watch how you drive — "feck sake." *(The guy gives him the finger. Brendan smiles. Gives the finger back.)* Yeah, you too.
WOMAN. At the moment, I'm going to my citizenship ceremony. Isn't that mad. Anyway, I better sign off. I'll write next month I promise. I just wanted to let you know I'm alright. I love you. Brendan. *(A small group of people are gathered as the Judge appears. They all have their right hands raised. Every character from the play but the Woman and Rose. They have their backs to the audience as the Judge stands on the podium, facing them. Brendan has his hand raised, too. He faces forward, though.)* P.S. I'll take a trip back sometime soon. *(The Woman remains in her seat as the lights come down on her. She slips off during the ceremony.)*

Scene 35

The Ceremony

The Big Hall — later. They put down their hands.

JUDGE 2. Of the twenty-six people here, twenty-three of you have changed your name to adopt the American phonetics. You have renounced the citizenship of your native country. You have overcome hurdles. You have overcome obstacles. You have been willing to change your identity, in many ways to become part of this nation, to become an American. And the sacrifices you have made are tremendous. But it is those sacrifices that will shape your new-found identity, and in your heart of hearts you may feel you are where you come from, but now you are what you choose, and you choose to be an American. Not an emigrant but a first-class citizen. And there are many who wish to stand where you stand today, and there are some who will hate you for standing there, because you are now a symbol of your nation, America: you are a symbol for equality, a symbol for liberty, and a symbol for the pursuit of happiness. And let me be the first to say — congratulations and welcome to your new home. *(We hear "The Star-Spangled Banner," and the celebratory confetti and flags drop as they congratulate each other. They all walk off. Brendan is alone. He brings his car to the front.)*

Scene 36

Coffee and a Donut

Rose enters. She is walking past the hall. Brendan sees her.

BRENDAN. Rose, I didn't expect you, to see you …
ROSE. I'm only here in, in, in, support for what you're doing. I watched it from the balcony.
BRENDAN. It's so good to see —
ROSE. Don't get any ideas. I'm still …
BRENDAN. I just wanted to tell you, I was a virgin before —
ROSE. I just want to say congratulations. That's all. I think it is commendable what you …
BRENDAN. I'm really glad you came. I really am. *(Pause.)*
ROSE. Well, I better —
BRENDAN. Would you like …
ROSE. What?
BRENDAN. It's okay. I don't want to put you —
ROSE. Yeah?
BRENDAN. I passed the driving test as well.
ROSE. Congratulations on that too. I'm sure you had a good teacher.
BRENDAN. Ah, Rose.
ROSE. Never mind, I shouldn't have said …
BRENDAN. You're very hard on me.
ROSE. Well, somebody has to be. *(Pause.)*
BRENDAN. I still have the tickets, you know. We could go —
ROSE. Brendan —
BRENDAN. I understand. Are you working later?
ROSE. No, I got the day off for —
BRENDAN. For the ceremony.
ROSE. Yeah.
BRENDAN. You don't want to waste it, you know.
ROSE. *(Smiles.)* You don't give in, do ya?
BRENDAN. Okay. I'm sorry for — was that a smile?

ROSE. No. What are you doing now?

BRENDAN. Well, I was thinking of going to the opera, but it doesn't mean the same without, thing, without …

ROSE. So, what are you doing?

BRENDAN. Oh, other stuff.

ROSE. Like?

BRENDAN. Well, I suppose I have to get something to eat. I didn't eat all morning. Very nervous.

ROSE. You didn't eat?

BRENDAN. We could get — maybe we might have time like, as a friend, even, just friends even —

ROSE. What?

BRENDAN. Well, to have maybe, some coffee or a donut.

ROSE. *(Smiles.)* Ohh, very American.

BRENDAN. I try.

ROSE. It's lunchtime now, you know.

BRENDAN. I suppose. For lunch. You wouldn't like to accompany me for lunch, that sounds so old-fashioned, accompany — There's a place around the corner. It will just be a celebratory meal or drink or … I'm a persistent Yank.

ROSE. About — the other — I wanted to say.

BRENDAN. *(Brushing it off and over her.)* Ah, it doesn't — it doesn't, you know

ROSE. I was, you know, I didn't mean. I mean, I just wanted to say, because I was thinking about it and I'm like, you know, whatever, like who am — you know, whatever, and that was another reason I came today — and I needed to say, I understand. I don't want you to get any ideas though. I just wanted. I needed to say, that. And ah, I just miss talking to you. A lot. You know.

BRENDAN. I'm just glad you're here.

ROSE. Fine.

BRENDAN. Fine … fine?

ROSE. Let's get something to eat.

BRENDAN. Together?

ROSE. Well, yeah.

BRENDAN. *(Smiling.)* I was thinking I could drive to the place if you want —

ROSE. It's only around the corner, you said —

BRENDAN. I know, but … I was thinking, you know, like, that it — It'll be fun.

ROSE. To drive?
BRENDAN. Yeah, in my car.
ROSE. Okay. *(Pause. We hear the early strains of Beethoven's "Pastoral" V. Allegretto [Shepherds' Song] from the Sixth Symphony.)* You're just lucky I like your accent.
BRENDAN. *(Smiling.)* I like your accent, too. *(Brendan opens the door for Rose. She acknowledges his gentlemanly behavior. She gets in. Brendan gets in the other side. He smiles his smile. We see his mother in silhouette, in the back, as she fades out. The music echoes all around as it plays, sweeping and clear. And as the lights go down, they drive on.)*

End of Play

PROPERTY LIST

Box of letters
Budweiser bottle
Harmonica
Cigarette, lighter
Jacket
Quarters
Whiskey, glass
Free newspaper with nudie cover
Personal phone book
2 Cars
Paintbrush, ladder
Lunch bag, food
"Roses" Irish chocolates
Money
Drink, watch, comb
Hershey's chocolate
Cup of tea
Bottle of pills
Notebook, pen
Large suitcase with wheels
Car side mirror
Steam iron, shirt, necktie
Envelope, opera tickets
Gift-wrapped CD
Letter, envelope

SOUND EFFECTS

Knocking at door
"Laudate Dominum" on car radio
Hard rock radio
Hip-hop music
"Barcarole" on boom box
Car alarm
Police car sirens
Car horn, plural horns
Above-ground train
All opera music as stated

NEW PLAYS

★ **GUARDIANS by Peter Morris.** In this unflinching look at war, a disgraced American soldier discloses the truth about Abu Ghraib prison, and a clever English journalist reveals how he faked a similar story for the London tabloids. "Compelling, sympathetic and powerful." *—NY Times.* "Sends you into a state of moral turbulence." *—Sunday Times (UK).* "Nothing short of remarkable." *—Village Voice.* [1M, 1W] ISBN: 978-0-8222-2177-7

★ **BLUE DOOR by Tanya Barfield.** Three generations of men (all played by one actor), from slavery through Black Power, challenge Lewis, a tenured professor of mathematics, to embark on a journey combining past and present. "A teasing flare for words." *—Village Voice.* "Unfailingly thought-provoking." *—LA Times.* "The play moves with the speed and logic of a dream." *—Seattle Weekly.* [2M] ISBN: 978-0-8222-2209-5

★ **THE INTELLIGENT DESIGN OF JENNY CHOW by Rolin Jones.** This irreverent "techno-comedy" chronicles one brilliant woman's quest to determine her heritage and face her fears with the help of her astounding creation called Jenny Chow. "Boldly imagined." *—NY Times.* "Fantastical and funny." *—Variety.* "Harvests many laughs and finally a few tears." *—LA Times.* [3M, 3W] ISBN: 978-0-8222-2071-8

★ **SOUVENIR by Stephen Temperley.** Florence Foster Jenkins, a wealthy society eccentric, suffers under the delusion that she is a great coloratura soprano—when in fact the opposite is true. "Hilarious and deeply touching. Incredibly moving and breathtaking." *—NY Daily News.* "A sweet love letter of a play." *—NY Times.* "Wildly funny. Completely charming." *—Star-Ledger.* [1M, 1W] ISBN: 978-0-8222-2157-9

★ **ICE GLEN by Joan Ackermann.** In this touching period comedy, a beautiful poetess dwells in idyllic obscurity on a Berkshire estate with a band of unlikely cohorts. "A beautifully written story of nature and change." *—Talkin' Broadway.* "A lovely play which will leave you with a lot to think about." *—CurtainUp.* "Funny, moving and witty." *—Metroland (Boston).* [4M, 3W] ISBN: 978-0-8222-2175-3

★ **THE LAST DAYS OF JUDAS ISCARIOT by Stephen Adly Guirgis.** Set in a time-bending, darkly comic world between heaven and hell, this play reexamines the plight and fate of the New Testament's most infamous sinner. "An unforced eloquence that finds the poetry in lowdown street talk." *—NY Times.* "A real jaw-dropper." *—Variety.* "An extraordinary play." *—Guardian (UK).* [10M, 5W] ISBN: 978-0-8222-2082-4

DRAMATISTS PLAY SERVICE, INC.
440 Park Avenue South, New York, NY 10016 212-683-8960 Fax 212-213-1539
postmaster@dramatists.com **www.dramatists.com**

NEW PLAYS

★ **THE GREAT AMERICAN TRAILER PARK MUSICAL music and lyrics by David Nehls, book by Betsy Kelso.** Pippi, a stripper on the run, has just moved into Armadillo Acres, wreaking havoc among the tenants of Florida's most exclusive trailer park. "Adultery, strippers, murderous ex-boyfriends, Costco and the Ice Capades. Undeniable fun." –*NY Post.* "Joyful and un-ashamedly vulgar." –*The New Yorker.* "Sparkles with treasure." –*New York Sun.* [2M, 5W] ISBN: 978-0-8222-2137-1

★ **MATCH by Stephen Belber.** When a young Seattle couple meet a promi-nent New York choreographer, they are led on a fraught journey that will change their lives forever. "Uproariously funny, deeply moving, enthralling theatre." –*NY Daily News.* "Prolific laughs and ear-to-ear smiles." –*NY Magazine.* [2M, 1W] ISBN: 978-0-8222-2020-6

★ **MR. MARMALADE by Noah Haidle.** Four-year-old Lucy's imaginary friend, Mr. Marmalade, doesn't have much time for her—not to mention he has a cocaine addiction and a penchant for pornography. "Alternately hilarious and heartbreaking." –*The New Yorker.* "A mature and accomplished play." –*LA Times.* "Scathingly observant comedy." –*Miami Herald.* [4M, 2W] ISBN: 978-0-8222-2142-5

★ **MOONLIGHT AND MAGNOLIAS by Ron Hutchinson.** Three men cloister themselves as they work tirelessly to reshape a screenplay that's just not working—*Gone with the Wind.* "Consumers of vintage Hollywood insider stories will eat up Hutchinson's diverting conjecture." –*Variety.* "A lot of fun." –*NY Post.* "A Hollywood dream-factory farce." –*Chicago Sun-Times.* [3M, 1W] ISBN: 978-0-8222-2084-8

★ **THE LEARNED LADIES OF PARK AVENUE by David Grimm, trans-lated and freely adapted from Molière's** *Les Femmes Savantes.* Dicky wants to marry Betty, but her mother's plan is for Betty to wed a most pompous man. "A brave, brainy and barmy revision." –*Hartford Courant.* "A rare but welcome bird in contemporary theatre." –*New Haven Register.* "Roll over Cole Porter." –*Boston Globe.* [5M, 5W] ISBN: 978-0-8222-2135-7

★ **REGRETS ONLY by Paul Rudnick.** A sparkling comedy of Manhattan manners that explores the latest topics in marriage, friendships and squandered riches. "One of the funniest quip-meisters on the planet." –*NY Times.* "Precious moments of hilarity. Devastatingly accurate political and social satire." –*BackStage.* "Great fun." –*CurtainUp.* [3M, 3W] ISBN: 978-0-8222-2223-1

DRAMATISTS PLAY SERVICE, INC.
440 Park Avenue South, New York, NY 10016 212-683-8960 Fax 212-213-1539
postmaster@dramatists.com www.dramatists.com

NEW PLAYS

★ **AFTER ASHLEY by Gina Gionfriddo.** A teenager is unwillingly thrust into the national spotlight when a family tragedy becomes talk-show fodder. "A work that virtually any audience would find accessible." *–NY Times.* "Deft characterization and caustic humor." *–NY Sun.* "A smart satirical drama." *–Variety.* [4M, 2W] ISBN: 978-0-8222-2099-2

★ **THE RUBY SUNRISE by Rinne Groff.** Twenty-five years after Ruby struggles to realize her dream of inventing the first television, her daughter faces similar battles of faith as she works to get Ruby's story told on network TV. "Measured and intelligent, optimistic yet clear-eyed." *–NY Magazine.* "Maintains an exciting sense of ingenuity." *–Village Voice.* "Sinuous theatrical flair." *–Broadway.com.* [3M, 4W] ISBN: 978-0-8222-2140-1

★ **MY NAME IS RACHEL CORRIE taken from the writings of Rachel Corrie, edited by Alan Rickman and Katharine Viner.** This solo piece tells the story of Rachel Corrie who was killed in Gaza by an Israeli bulldozer set to demolish a Palestinian home. "Heartbreaking urgency. An invigoratingly detailed portrait of a passionate idealist." *–NY Times.* "Deeply authentically human." *–USA Today.* "A stunning dramatization." *–CurtainUp.* [1W] ISBN: 978-0-8222-2222-4

★ **ALMOST, MAINE by John Cariani.** This charming midwinter night's dream of a play turns romantic clichés on their ear as it chronicles the painfully hilarious amorous adventures (and misadventures) of residents of a remote northern town that doesn't quite exist. "A whimsical approach to the joys and perils of romance." *–NY Times.* "Sweet, poignant and witty." *–NY Daily News.* "Aims for the heart by way of the funny bone." *–Star-Ledger.* [2M, 2W] ISBN: 978-0-8222-2156-2

★ **Mitch Albom's TUESDAYS WITH MORRIE by Jeffrey Hatcher and Mitch Albom, based on the book by Mitch Albom.** The true story of Brandeis University professor Morrie Schwartz and his relationship with his student Mitch Albom. "A touching, life-affirming, deeply emotional drama." *–NY Daily News.* "You'll laugh. You'll cry." *–Variety.* "Moving and powerful." *–NY Post.* [2M] ISBN: 978-0-8222-2188-3

★ **DOG SEES GOD: CONFESSIONS OF A TEENAGE BLOCKHEAD by Bert V. Royal.** An abused pianist and a pyromaniac ex-girlfriend contribute to the teen-angst of America's most hapless kid. "A welcome antidote to the notion that the *Peanuts* gang provides merely American cuteness." *–NY Times.* "Hysterically funny." *–NY Post.* "The *Peanuts* kids have finally come out of their shells." *–Time Out.* [4M, 4W] ISBN: 978-0-8222-2152-4

DRAMATISTS PLAY SERVICE, INC.
440 Park Avenue South, New York, NY 10016 212-683-8960 Fax 212-213-1539
postmaster@dramatists.com www.dramatists.com

NEW PLAYS

★ **RABBIT HOLE by David Lindsay-Abaire.** Winner of the 2007 Pulitzer Prize. Becca and Howie Corbett have everything a couple could want until a life-shattering accident turns their world upside down. "An intensely emotional examination of grief, laced with wit." *–Variety.* "A transcendent and deeply affecting new play." *–Entertainment Weekly.* "Painstakingly beautiful." *–BackStage.* [2M, 3W] ISBN: 978-0-8222-2154-8

★ **DOUBT, A Parable by John Patrick Shanley.** Winner of the 2005 Pulitzer Prize and Tony Award. Sister Aloysius, a Bronx school principal, takes matters into her own hands when she suspects the young Father Flynn of improper relations with one of the male students. "All the elements come invigoratingly together like clockwork." *–Variety.* "Passionate, exquisite, important, engrossing." *–NY Newsday.* [1M, 3W] ISBN: 978-0-8222-2219-4

★ **THE PILLOWMAN by Martin McDonagh.** In an unnamed totalitarian state, an author of horrific children's stories discovers that someone has been making his stories come true. "A blindingly bright black comedy." *–NY Times.* "McDonagh's least forgiving, bravest play." *–Variety.* "Thoroughly startling and genuinely intimidating." *–Chicago Tribune.* [4M, 5 bit parts (2M, 1W, 1 boy, 1 girl)] ISBN: 978-0-8222-2100-5

★ **GREY GARDENS book by Doug Wright, music by Scott Frankel, lyrics by Michael Korie.** The hilarious and heartbreaking story of Big Edie and Little Edie Bouvier Beale, the eccentric aunt and cousin of Jacqueline Kennedy Onassis, once bright names on the social register who became East Hampton's most notorious recluses. "An experience no passionate theatergoer should miss." *–NY Times.* "A unique and unmissable musical." *–Rolling Stone.* [4M, 3W, 2 girls] ISBN: 978-0-8222-2181-4

★ **THE LITTLE DOG LAUGHED by Douglas Carter Beane.** Mitchell Green could make it big as the hot new leading man in Hollywood if Diane, his agent, could just keep him in the closet. "Devastatingly funny." *–NY Times.* "An out-and-out delight." *–NY Daily News.* "Full of wit and wisdom." *–NY Post.* [2M, 2W] ISBN: 978-0-8222-2226-2

★ **SHINING CITY by Conor McPherson.** A guilt-ridden man reaches out to a therapist after seeing the ghost of his recently deceased wife. "Haunting, inspired and glorious." *–NY Times.* "Simply breathtaking and astonishing." *–Time Out.* "A thoughtful, artful, absorbing new drama." *–Star-Ledger.* [3M, 1W] ISBN: 978-0-8222-2187-6

DRAMATISTS PLAY SERVICE, INC.
440 Park Avenue South, New York, NY 10016 212-683-8960 Fax 212-213-1539
postmaster@dramatists.com www.dramatists.com